BECAUSE JAPAN
日本ですから

A tell-all memoir of life in Tokyo

ASH WATSON

To Nisa, it was so lovely to meet you!

CRANTHORPE
MILLNER

A CIP catalogue record for this title is available from the British Library.

ISBN 978-1-912964-33-8 (Paperback)

www.cranthorpemillner.com

First Published (2020)

Cranthorpe Millner Publishers

出る釘は打たれる。まあ、私は目立つけど。

"The nail that stands out must be hammered down.
Well, I stand out!"

CONTENTS

目次

AUTHOR'S NOTE

The names of individuals have been used with full consent from each person. Destination reviews have been intentionally left out for fear of sounding like a tour guide, as, with any expatriate, emotions work like rollercoasters and influence any encounter or experience. It must therefore be noted that all reports have been written purely for entertainment value and are by no means there to influence or persuade the reader otherwise.

INTRODUCTION

前置き

Tens of thousands of people were running as one along the beach, boardwalk and grass verge, in my direction. I was sitting directly in their trajectory and had to move.

I immediately jumped up and assumed, in this setting, the only reasonable explanation was that a tsunami warning had been issued, which had, in my moment of mindfulness, completely bypassed me.

My mind went into overdrive as I tried to recall the ten-minute what-to-do-in-a-tsunami tutorial I received during my initial job orientation six weeks prior. They issued us pocket sized earthquake and tsunami guides to carry at all times. In this precise moment of need, it laid safely on my kitchen table under a pile of paperwork.

Useful.

Deciding I only had one real option, I began to sprint at full speed, intertwining between the fleeing masses towards higher ground. I was now part of the stampede. Images of wildebeest flowing into a ravine towards a young lion cub sprung to mind.

"Where are we heading?" I wondered. "There must be a safehouse or school nearby that we are being evacuated to."

What happened next stunned me, as the reason behind the tsunami soon became clear...

***

I first visited Japan in the summer of 2005 on a foreign exchange programme with my high school. I instantly fell in love with the culture, the vibrancy, the food and the atmosphere. I returned every couple of years, to visit friends and travel to new destinations, until 2016 when I received an offer to teach English in a high school, and decided to quit my current job at a Veterinary Referrals Practice and hop on a plane.

Japan had always been at the back of my mind and the indescribable feeling that I gleaned from being there was what kept dragging me back. I always felt a wistful sense of belonging, and despite what many may think, it took me to simpler times, when daily worries were minimal and just 'being' was at the forefront of daily life.

I have spent many years trying to explain this euphoric mind-set to my peers, and so after two years of living in such a wonderful place, I have decided to commit to paper what it was really like. It was as much a journey of personal growth as a time in which I learned about the intricacies of Japanese culture.

What follows is an account of my time in Japan, the day-to-day scenarios I found myself in and the observations I made of the culture and traditions.

A previous boss, mentor and friend of mine gifted me with a beautiful leather journal before I left the UK and I decided to bestow upon it the honour of becoming my 'Journal of Firsts': first encounters, first experiences, first pilgrimages, first thoughts on important or horrific moments.

I always kept travel journals whenever I travelled abroad to keep my memories alive and true. Keeping this new Journal of Firsts not only allowed me to document and reflect upon things I deemed vital in the moment, but, in order to keep it interesting, it also encouraged me to get out into the world, step out of my comfort zone, and experience things I would have not usually experienced.

My habit of keeping travel journals began the first time I visited Japan. I travelled up and down the country with eight students, and our teacher instructed us to keep diaries as a souvenir of our journeys together. It also allowed us to truly appreciate and savour each day as it came. We would tape envelopes of all sizes to the inside of both covers to collect ticket stubs, train tickets, leaflets and flyers from each place we visited, maps and a multitude of origami.

I liked this idea and revelled at the memento of my time there so much that I continued the habit into adulthood. I currently own four journals for Japan, as well as one each for America, Australia, Mauritius and Taiwan. I turned them into mini scrap books, utilising all my collected ticket stubs, leaflets and photos throughout, and very much enjoy reliving the experiences each time I read them.

I hope you enjoy this journey as much as I have.

1
SHOUGANAI

しょうがない

Sitting down to allow my mind to reflect on why I left the UK and what I encountered early on in my Japanese life has been a fun and challenging feat. Japan is the country that does not stop giving and yet somehow takes a part of you with it. Upon relocation, my lifelong opinions were disregarded in an instant and unknown emotions presented themselves at unexpected occasions.

Nothing was what I thought it would be and many things were surprisingly better than I could have ever imagined. The things I missed from home were replaced by newfound loves, and rage-inducing nuisances became trivial anecdotes. New obsessions took a hold of old ones and obliterated them in blurs of mochi, gachapon and azuki beans.

I moved to Japan to live in the land that does not judge; where crime rates and bins do not exist, and though the majority of what I first thought proved true, I was in for a plethora of wake-up calls as gradually the utopia I came to call home cracked at the seams and revealed itself for what it truly was. Was this a bad thing? In hindsight, I now know it to be a typical case of the dreaded 'Culture Shock', something I was ignorant enough to believe I knew enough about to avoid completely.

In life, I truly welcome mistakes, as they encourage growth and wisdom, but sometimes misguided thoughts and expectations can cause irrefutable side effects.

One misjudgement on my part opened a whole Pandora's box of drama just a few days after arrival when I was shopping at a local supermarket.

My first two days in Japan were spent at an intense training orientation programme in a fancy 5-star hotel in Shinjuku, giving me and my new colleagues no time to truly soak in our new surroundings and explore the city. Thereafter, I was placed in temporary accommodation in Ikebukuro, allowing me to slowly integrate into a semi-normal lifestyle.

Feeling slightly overwhelmed by the uncertainty of my new life, one thing I looked forward to was my weekly food shopping adventure, where I could focus on something I knew, something I could handle with ease. I thought.

Each time I visited the supermarket, I would aim to buy something new and random to sample that evening. The weirder the better. After a while I even got to know the staff working behind the tills, as they would comment on the strange and unrelated menagerie of items I purchased.

6

Each limited or seasonal food item would make its way into my basket and the cashiers would giggle at my obvious excitement to shove it in my face. All the new flavours of tea, Calpis and Fanta began to wear thin after a while, however, and I decided the best solution was to find some good old trusty squash (fruit cordial drink) to calm my thirst.

As I strolled up and down the aisles excited for a little home comfort, it occurred to me that I'd never actually seen squash, or heard any mention of it in any shape or form during my many visits to Japan. Frantic, I immediately turned to Google in search of 'squash drink in Tokyo' and to my astonishment, no such thing exists (in the western sense that is; there is a fizzy lemon drink called Squash which upset me greatly for its false advertisement).

How could it be possible, with all the weird and wonderful flavour combinations and beverages available, that such a common household staple simply never made its way over to the east?

Standing in the middle of the busy supermarket aisle, suddenly nothing else in life mattered. The whole day, nay, my entire life in Japan was ruined. Perspective and reasoning were unfathomable and I found myself in the middle of an existential crisis. I felt utterly overwhelmed as I stood there surrounded by looping nonsensical jingles advertising eggs and bento boxes, choruses of "IRASSHAIMASE" from the clerks as they wheeled around new produce, and streams of undiscovered sea creatures staring up at me through glazed eyes from the chilled iced boxes.

My heart began to race exponentially and at once it dawned on me that possibly my reaction was somewhat irrational.

Did it truly matter that Japan didn't hold supplies of squash?

Well, actually, yes.

But were my reactions overzealous?

Again, yes.

So, what was the cure to this epidemic? Well I turned to a Japanese friend for the answer, and after explaining my plight, was rewarded with a single word. One word that summed up all the worries and stressors in my life. One magical expression that at once seemed to irradiate any anxiety or ill feelings. What was this word?

Shouganai.

If somebody had said to me, "It can't be helped" or, "There's nothing you can do about it" in English, it would have enraged me, but for some reason this dulcet sounding word had enough charm and expression attached to it that it actually worked.

I mean, yes, I still ranted to my friends back home as if my world had ended, and yes, they sent me over a delightful parcel of squash to placate my woes, but for that day at least, my new favourite mantra in life saved me from one miserable afternoon and gave me a thrilling new tale for my Journal of Firsts.

The first time I experienced culture shock.

2
TRAIN CHRONICLES #1

電車物語# 1

Standard

As I rode to work during my first week, it occurred to me just how much of an important role trains play in the daily lives of the Japanese. As with any aspect of Japanese life, trains are shrouded in rules and regulations, some of which may not exist in the west, and most of which I only came to realise myself after living through many vital errors.

On my daily commutes, I had begun to slowly pick up on some of these rules and most importantly the social mistakes. I was usually never divulged in person of any wrongdoings, but instead would be subject to an onslaught of subtly disapproving glares.

Tourists in their masses flooded Tokyo each day utilising standards of etiquette and social norms from their native homelands. Locals were accommodating to a certain extent, and made leeway through kindness; ignoring groups of excitable expats talking loudly and playing music on their devices. Having lived there only a few weeks, I was already realising the true art, beauty and majesty of the rail system.

As with any large city, there were peak and off-peak times to use and avoid the trains, but with the ever-growing population within the mega city of Tokyo, locals had adopted a more precise set of standards that appeared almost innate.

As you will find out in the coming chapters, stepping through the sliding doors, societal norms were no longer construct, and it could easily become a ruthless world of passive-aggressive politeness. During my many visits to Japan in the past, I had grown accustomed to the trains in a way, but this was of course during a time when access to a mobile phone with internet was non-existent, so instead I focused all my time on reading maps and enjoying the novelty of it all. People would stare a lot, but I was adorned in full Japan-tourist attire; backpack, walking shoes, camera x 3 [LSR, Polaroid and Go Pro (Yes, I was THAT guy)], so it didn't bother me as attention would have been drawn in any setting.

So, let's back track and return to the station entrance.

Each line on the JR (Japan Railway) or Metro is signified with its own colour and signs which are plentiful and often written in at least Japanese and English (often Chinese and Korean too), so stations are extremely easy to navigate for most visitors.

Using either JR or Metro, I would always recommend that passengers embrace the use of the IC card. I had figured out that I could use either SUICA or PASMO, both of which were available from most machines inside the stations, just outside of the ticket gates.

I was issued a commuter's SUICA card. This gave me free transport between my home and the station closest to my work, which was particularly useful on my days off.

As I arrived at my station each morning, I would swipe through the gates and navigate my way to the correct platform, standing in line by the carriage doors. I noticed that people lined in twos and as the train approached, split and relocated to either side of the opening doors, allowing the passengers to alight safely.

I was surprised that, unlike in London, people did not begin pushing as soon as the doors opened, but instead, everybody was allowed to disembark with patience. I noticed passengers already on the train, looking around to see if anybody needed to get off, and if the carriage was too busy, they themselves stepped off to allow others to do so.

Boarding the train, I began to take in the various areas there were to choose from. There were the main seats (the ends being the most desired spots), the priority seats in the corners of each carriage, the foyer where those not travelling far would stand patiently, and the aisle where those on for the long haul lined carefully in front of seated passengers.

The station jingle played as the doors finally closed, allowing those late comers to jump in at the last second. Each area of Tokyo has its own distinct station platform jingle; some are of historical significance, some are famous Japanese melodies and others are bird noises or polyphonic tones reminiscent of those old noughties phone sounds kids used to play on the buses. Some trains will even blare a mix of deer snorts and dog barks whilst moving to deter wild animals from straying onto the tracks.

The TV systems differed on each line, but most displayed information on the upcoming station, alongside advertisements of all kinds. So the trains were extremely easy to fathom, and if I couldn't catch the display in time, the conductor or pre-recorded message would soon announce the next station and which side the doors were going to open.

Japanese trains are notoriously punctual and often display messages of apologies for being late with a multitude of explanations for each journey. They are, in fact, constantly displayed regardless of suspension and I have, over the years, noted the weird and wonderful excuses for the trains being delayed:

Signal inspection, signal trouble, blackout, congestion, safety check, clearing tracks, cable problems, car inspection, customer fall, on-board inspection, trouble on board, obstacle thing (yes it truly said thing), person entry, person relief, person injury, passenger rescue, human body accident, trouble on board, wheel skidding, wind, typhoon, tree, snow, and my personal favourite, antelope.

I even heard announcements mentioning dog on track, conductor forgot or lost keys, conductor's glasses blown away by the wind, bird and wild boar collision with train, and believe it or not, vegetables on tracks!

Sitting on the train was a real treat and sometimes making the effort to walk to the first carriage to escape the crowds paid off. When I first arrived in Japan I had a real trouble with train paranoia. I would become extremely aware of people staring at me and of those who refused to sit next to me. Passengers would move to the end of the row when a space became available and I would often take it to heart, thinking perhaps I smelt or they were uncomfortable sitting next to a foreigner.

The fact that speaking loudly or talking on the phones is strictly prohibited in Japan only increased my paranoia because I never knew what people were thinking. I would often find myself standing or sitting in complete silence, all the while wondering if people were silently hating me for some unknown offence.

After a few months of observing this behaviour however, I brought the topic to a Japanese friend who assured me that those end seats are the best on-board and people will rush to be seated there. As for the staring, it was all part of being a foreigner in Japan. People would stare, talk about me

14

directly in front of me and even take pictures. I soon became accustomed to this and only rarely did it intrude on my life.

Whether I love them or hate them, trains became a huge part of my daily life in Japan and were the setting for many an encounter that I jotted down in my Journal of Firsts.

3
TADAIMA PART ONE

ただいま#1

The Hunt

As previously mentioned, my company kindly put me up in a temporary apartment in West Ikebukuro for the first two weeks whilst I settled myself into my new surroundings. It was not in the nicest of areas I came to find out (cue the red-light district and massage parlours that offer happy endings - I did not try either!), but either way, it gave me a halfway home and a base in which to organise my new life.

The apartment itself was everything I needed in one bite-size space. The door opened to a narrow arm-span width kitchen with a washroom off to the side; the kitchen led into a small bedroom big enough for a double bed, small dining set and a TV unit. The balcony overlooked the train tracks and a labyrinth of karaoke bars and pachinko parlours below.

I was just a five-minute walk to a huge shopping mall called Sunshine City (that famously held the Tokyo Mega

Pokémon Centre), which elated me muchly upon arrival. I was comfortable there and soon realised that this was all a person in my situation required for a happy life. This realisation only occurred in hindsight however, and my greedy British self first walked into an estate agents with entirely different ideas and expectations.

I was recommended by some expat friends to go through a particular foreign-friendly estate agent and guarantor company. They also offered a phone contract service which would prevent me the drama of trying to set up one on my own accord (as I've heard it can be a total mission for foreigners in Japan). So, that is what I did.

I contacted the real estate before arriving in Tokyo, and set up a meeting with them on my third day in town. I boarded the Yamanote Line; Tokyo's only circle line, and headed off with excitement and apprehension. (Many drunken people famously take advantage of the Yamanote's service by boarding, falling asleep for an hour and waking up in the same station they just left, allowing their unconscious body to tour the circumference of the mega city undaunted.)

I arrived in Shin-Okubo, also known as Korea Town, and was instantly transported into a district that excited all my senses at once. I was overcome with the sounds of K-pop blasting from every shop, window and car. My nose and taste buds were picking up notes of BBQs and spices I'd never tasted before. My eyes struggled to choose one thing to focus on through the menagerie of flashing lights, signs and food stalls, and my sense of touch... well the streets were thin as hell so I expected to be shoved left, right and centre in order to move anywhere (I had perfected the art of tensing my arms to push any brave on-comers out of my way).

Attempting to go there during the rain was a risky business as people's lack of spatial awareness mixed with the addition of a huge umbrella was an eyeball's worst nightmare. I thanked the heavens for my poor vision every time it rained as my glasses saved me from a lobotomy on an hourly basis.

After walking up and down the same street for almost half an hour unable to find the estate agent, I had finally caught all that Pokémon Go had to offer in the area and decided to call the agency who directed me to a tiny sign in a third storey window, along with a well-hidden staircase amongst food stands and bicycle parking bays.

Climbing the winding stairs, I was greeted by a chorus of "IRASHAIMASE" before being guided to a seat where my new Korean estate agent came over to introduce himself. (For the sake of anonymity, I shall refer to him as 'Jin'.)

Prior to flying to Japan, the agency had advised me to use their website in order to browse and select a few apartments to view on the day of our initial meeting to maximise the time we had to view each place.

My workplace was located in North Tokyo, so I chose ten apartments in Northern Tokyo and Southern Saitama, the next prefecture outside Tokyo. Jin informed me that eight out of the ten apartments I had selected had rejected me without question because of my foreign status. He told me that it was illegal practice within Japan to reject people based on race alone, but all landlords did it anyway. In fact, it was extremely commonplace, even if said foreigners could communicate in Japanese fluently and had lived in the country for many years. This both surprised and angered me as I had expected more of Japan, especially within my first few days.

Lesson One learned.

He informed me that he had called around and spoken to over twenty different landlords, only three of which would even consider letting to foreigners. Even those three required a lot of persuading; the selling point was that a Japanese company would be my guarantor should anything go wrong.

So, my first adventure into Japanese real estate began. We headed first to Warabi station in Saitama. Jin spent the entire journey regaling me with stories of his life, all centred around how much he hated Japan and Japanese people. He was a recent newlywed and father, and was explaining how he hated his new life and that I should never marry or have children because they sucked away your life. He was very unhappy in Japan and was planning on moving back to Korea as soon as possible.

I thought him both hilarious and quite frank, and respected

this because he was the first honest person I'd encountered since landing. Furthermore I was desperate for his help and under huge time restraints, so held my tongue where I would usually convey my concern.

The first apartment we visited was around fifteen minutes' walk from the station which I thought was really close. It transpired that for Japanese people this was a pilgrimage. Coming from the UK where virtually nobody outside of London uses the train system, I was pleased with the walking distance. This fact was met with a stunned response from Jin.

The apartment was on the third storey and was huge in comparison to other Japanese apartments I had previously stayed in. It was at least four times the size of my temporary apartment in Ikebukuro. I instantly fell in love as it was exactly what I was looking for: a spare room, a separate bathroom and toilet, in a quiet area and enough room to actually move around.

I decided not to jump on this one right away and continued on to see the other three places Jin had lined up. The second wasn't too far away but was a twenty-minute walk, ten-minute bus ride and then another fifteen-minute train ride to my work. I knew this would be impractical and grow quite tiresome after the novelty of moving there had worn off.

The place itself was perfect. It was really open and well lit, with a brand-new built-in kitchen area including a stove. There was a window hatch from the kitchen into the living area which opened it up even more. A walk-in closet was situated in one of the bedrooms and the balcony overlooked an allotment where I could imagine myself stealing fruit and vegetables from the local neighbours whilst striking up a pleasant intercultural and language exchange.

I envisioned my entire stay in Japan happily living in this place. The door even opened up on the ground floor and looked onto my own private staircase up to the first floor. It was very clean, spacious and open. Everything I wanted except the mission it would take to get anywhere. We were sweating buckets just trying to find this place in the summer heat, I could barely imagine trekking this journey day in day out in my formal work attire.

After a brief stop at the local combini (a convenience store like 7 Eleven, Family Mart and Lawson, found on every street corner) for an ice-cream break, Jin and I headed to the third place which was just around the corner from the second. It was in a more built up area and was much more compact. Each of the three places had either two bedrooms and a separate kitchen/dining area or one master bedroom with a spare room that could be used as a living room or bedroom, then a small kitchenette in the same room. I wasn't as blown away by the third one as I was the first two.

Jin walked away for a bit to give me time to collect my thoughts and make comparisons on each one. I had been taking short videos of each place on my phone as I walked around each, so I could accurately remember them. He came back and told me he had just received a call from the

21

office stating that they had two more for us to look around. The first was tiny and cheap and the second was in the same building as the first place that I really liked.

I decided to skip the former and we headed to the building from the first one to view the apartment beneath the original. It was a tiny bit cheaper but the layout was less open than the first. After seeing the other three places I decided that the first apartment was the one for me.

I wasn't exactly sure of its precise location as I was still to get a phone contract, but I knew it was only fifteen minutes by train from work and a fifteen-minute walk to the train station. Jin told me it was really close to the centre of Tokyo and that sold it for me.

I asked to venture upstairs once more to check out my future apartment. I now saw it through different eyes. I saw the potential of what this place could be. The afternoon sun cast long columns of orange light across the wooden floor, and I imagined where my bed and table would stand. I imagined friends I didn't yet have coming for dinner parties in the evenings and friends from the UK staying in the spare room.

We went for a gyoza lunch nearby and discussed our lives. Jin told me how much he disliked Japan once more and we joked and laughed about his misery. I thought he was simply joking at first but then he started to tell me how homesick he felt. I felt bad for him and thought maybe he just needed someone to vent to, even if it was a little unprofessional.

Later on, that afternoon, we arrived back at the office to go through all the paperwork. Luckily, the apartment I had chosen didn't require any deposit (usually a month's rent) or key money (an unnecessarily mandatory gift to the landlord that is usually around a month's rent also). I just had to pay a month's rent up front and they wouldn't charge me in the following month.

I was told that my contract was for two-years and that I could cancel easily at any time; all I would need to do is give a month's notice and pay the cleaning fees when I leave. I thought this was a brilliant deal so signed and stamped the contract with my hanko (wooden seal depicting your name, used to sign documents instead of a pen) there and then.

I also signed up for a phone contract through them as they offered a good service to foreigners with a friendly, English help service. I bought an unlocked iPhone SE before coming to Japan so all I needed was a Japanese SIM card to use. They signed me up with their private phone network which shared its name with the popular company Docomo.

So, that was that. One day, four apartments and a phone contract later, I had somewhere to live, almost. Both my mother and I just had to endure a brief phone interview to prove that I was who I said I was, and it was done. I felt a mixture of pride in myself for overcoming this huge milestone, and relief for ticking off the largest box on my ever-growing to-do list.

I had a two-day cross over period with my temporary apartment allowing me to move my luggage over at my own pace. I had arranged for the gas and water to be turned on the day that I arrived, and was also recommended to use a second-hand appliance refurbishing company to buy my big appliances from. I accepted their offer and paid ¥10,000 (£75) for a microwave, stove, refrigerator and washing machine. The guy also installed them as part of the charge. In total my fees for the day were ¥278,545 (£1,820) for the first month's rent, the agency and guarantor fees, buying and installing the appliances, and my phone contract for that month.

The next step was to sort out the internet. My Japanese friend took me to Docomo a few days later to help me set up my connection with them. They operated solely in Japanese and therefore only accepted customers who spoke and understood Japanese well. My technical and formal Japanese wasn't very good at the time so I definitely needed someone there to help me.

They asked which phone company I was with because existing customers didn't have to pay the ¥38,000 (£250) installation fee. I told them I was with Docomo (which, upon seeing the small 'Docomo' sign in the corner of my screen, they believed, even though technically I was with the fake Docomo). After almost two hours going through pages and pages of tedious documents, they told me I had been accepted and that they would come to my house in a month's time.

Then began the quietest month of my life. I was completely cut off from the outside world. I opted for the lowest data scheme with my phone and needed to save all my data for Google Maps and Pokémon Go (naturally). It wasn't until October that the internet man came and saved my life. He arrived, installed and left in one swift movement that lasted all but fifteen minutes. My saviour.

This brings us nicely onto the apartment itself. It was on the third and top floor of a small block of about fifteen apartments. The entrance was nicely hidden away in a small cul-de-sac in a residential area on the West side of Warabi. It was situated between a retirement home and an elementary school, so occasionally I would be awoken abruptly by an ambulance in the middle of the night blaring its sirens and loudspeakers to all who were sleeping soundly. I never understood the necessity to advertise their arrival.

In the outdoor lobby area on the ground floor, we each had our own combination locked post box. This saved the postman a trip to each floor, even though they loved to hand things to me in person, whether it be a tiny envelope or huge box.

Opening my front door, I entered the genkan, or Japanese entrance way. It's a small tiled area where I would be expected to remove my outer shoes and don my inner shoes. I never used house shoes so just deposited my shoes in the shoe cupboard provided. Walking up the little step onto the linoleum wooden floors, I walked through another door into the kitchen.

Japanese apartments are measured in square metres and are categorised into room numbers. For example, a 1LDK is a single room with all living space plus kitchen combined together (no matter the kind of apartment there is always a separate washroom). A 1K has one room and a separate, small kitchen. A 1DK is larger than a 1K and has one bedroom and one kitchen/dining room. The average size of a one-person Japanese apartment in Tokyo was around 20m^2 and can cost anywhere from around ¥60,000 (£425) upwards.

I lived in a 2DK, which was 40.72m^2 and my rent was ¥69,000 (£490) plus ¥4000 (£30) management fees, so before bills and everything else my monthly payments were ¥73,000 (£482). That was a really good price considering the location and its size.

My spacious kitchen was big enough to run around in. I had a small kitchenette with a sink, draining board/prep area, and a small camping stove. Japanese apartments do not come fitted with an oven and I was lucky to find one with a fitted stove. I purchased a dining table which I rarely used, but was nice when guests came over.

There were four doors in my kitchen: Door One led back to the genkan, Door Two led to the washroom area on the left (next to which were two sliding doors parallel to the front door, each leading into a separate room), Door Three led to the living room on the left and finally Door Four led to the bedroom on the right.

Walking through Door Two, I entered a small space that held my washing machine. Straight ahead was my separate WC where my beautiful Japanese toilet sat. That beast came equipped with a menagerie of buttons that sprayed water into every orifice; I could also control the water jet power and the temperature of the seat. This came in particularly handy in the winter months. On top of the toilet was a built-in sink that ran when flushed. This method of recycling water was so ingenious that I do not understand why it has never been implemented in the west.

If I took the folding door to the right, I entered the bathroom/wet room. The floors and walls were all plastic and waterproof. A mirror hung above the sink that split the room in two. The faucet could be directed both into the sink and into the bath to fill it up. The bath was tiny, about half the size of a western bath, but almost twice as deep. I had a shower on the wall that enabled me to stand up and wash rather that bathe all the time (even though I adore taking baths so would squeeze myself into my little green box whenever I could).

Traditionally in Japan, you are expected to wash yourself outside the bath, then get in the constantly hot water to bathe (or squish yourself in with bent knees) and (try to) relax. This water can often be controlled by a device on the wall and is emptied once a week or so. I never owned such a device so used this room the western way.

As I said, Door Three led to the living room. This room was my traditional Japanese room with six tatami mats on the floor. When I first moved in the smell was amazing; reminiscent of those long summer days spent in the countryside, climbing on top of hay bales and rolling them down the hill. I loved the idea of having these at first, until I discovered the drama with the upkeep of them. They had to be hand cleaned regularly, never allowed to get wet, and constantly checked for mites and other small critters. This room had a big wooden built-in closet with long room-length shelves.

To enter my bedroom I could either use Door Four from the kitchen or the sliding doors dividing the two rooms down the middle. This room was the same size as the living room, except there was no closet space. The floor in there was wooden (and dented easily so furniture socks were a must!).

Finally, at the back of the apartment ran my apartment-length balcony. Floor-length glass sliding doors (with one screen door on each side) ran along my bedroom and living room. Stepping outside I had a view of the top of Warabi and directly below stood the retirement home. I could see my supermarket in the distance and in the spring the streets were lined with Sakura trees. It was a nice neighbourhood, and one that was usually quiet all year around.

It was not the best home in the world and it may have only been a fraction of the size of my house back in the UK, but it was safe, and it was home, and most importantly, it was mine.

4

TRAIN CHRONICLES #2

電車物語#2

The Invader

Animals are prohibited on the train system in Japan unless they are under ten kilograms and are kept in a small pet case, so you can only imagine my shock when I noticed something non-human moving on board.

Riding the train to Yoyogi one morning I peered up and directed my gaze towards a young woman sitting opposite me. A pretty standard sight graced me; she was playing on her phone and ignoring everyone else around her. This didn't interest me so I began to look around the carriage, taking in my surroundings until my peripherals picked up something twitching.

My eyes flickered back to the woman and down towards her legs where I spotted something sinister making its way in the direction of her knees. A big black and hairy, palm-sized spider was traversing her tights and swiftly heading northwards.

The young victim was in business attire and was clutching

her bag tightly upon her lap, making her blissfully unaware of the hiking invader. Its spindly legs twisted and turned as it hooked onto the edge of her skirt and began to circle around to find its bearings, all the while I am sitting there, hopelessly watching and praying that by chance the young woman looks down.

The spider wasn't a fan of resting and was soon unhooking its legs from the hem of her skirt and motioning towards the dark shadows of the underside of her lap. In an instance I was overcome with a sense of protection from the injustice and was grappling between fight or flight, ignore or act. The spider was taunting me and this poor innocent woman was none the wiser.

I had to act. It was now or never.

More passengers boarded the train and began to stand in between us both, shielding my vision. Out of sight, out of mind? No, I couldn't allow such a travesty to unfold any further. The inner chivalrous knight in me dropped my bag, leapt forward through strangers' legs and dove at the young woman's knees.

I quickly realised she was wearing earphones and couldn't hear my warning. I tried to get her attention by waving and shouting spider in Japanese, but this only panicked her further. She looked both baffled and terrified at the sight of the strange man crouching at her knees and waving like a madman. Finally, after what seemed like hours of pointing at her lap to get her attention, the realisation of my intention

31

began to show on her face and I took the opportunity to swat with all the power I could muster in the direction of the culprit.

I caught it on the first attempt, and it flew off her legs and across the carriage. If this didn't make her realise my intent was innocent, nothing would, and she gave out a little squeal of fear, shock and gratitude as finally all became clear. She bowed her head to thank me as I reversed back through the legs and into my seat, collecting my bag on the way.

As I straightened myself, I suddenly felt the dozens of eyes all staring at me and could feel my face turning a deep shade of scarlet. Thankfully, the other passengers had caught on much quicker than the young woman and to my relief and surprise, some began clapping at my chivalry which was halted by the realisation that the spider was still at large somewhere in the carriage.

At the next stop, looking frantically around, the majority of the remaining passengers either left or moved into the next carriage as the spider's next victim entered the train. I located it as it peered out from under the chairs opposite. Thus began phase two as he headed towards another young woman standing with her boyfriend in the entrance of the carriage.

My heart couldn't handle this again; I was simply on my way to the park to sunbathe with some friends. I didn't ask to enter the realms of wildlife ranger. The creature eyed the new girl up and made its way through unsuspecting feet towards her legs, not stopping as it clambered swiftly up her shoes. It struggled for a second on the smooth surface but managed to hook its leg in the opening above her ankle.

Thankfully this girl was not wearing any tights and the spider was barely half-way up her calf when she felt the sensation, twitched, peered down and screamed as she kicked it off like a bucking bronco. Her boyfriend tried to stamp at the fiend but was too slow and it retreated back under the seats ready for its next prey.

As I exited the train a few stops later, the first girl stood up, bowed once more and thanked me for saving her.

"All in a day's work!" I thought as I headed toward the park for a well-deserved drink... or six.

5

TADAIMA PART TWO

ただいま#2

Nesting

On the first day in my shiny new apartment, with help from a new work colleague, I travelled to the local (three stations and an hour walk away) Nitori (Japanese home store) to purchase a futon and some bedding. We traipsed for miles in the 40-degree heat, sweating profusely, and didn't return home until late that evening.

We set up my new futon, cracked open an alcoholic beverage and an ice-cream and sat on my balcony to listen to the cicadas as the sun set. Walking back into the pitch-black apartment later on, it dawned on me that there were no light bulbs in the sockets. At all. That this basic requirement would be provided was something that I had completely taken for granted. It was both a nuisance and a source of amusement.

My co-worker went home and I was left in the darkness

34

with just my laptop to light my way. I decided to walk to
the local combini to buy some bulbs and after speaking to
an American woman who was also shopping, discovered
that I cannot use everyday bulbs, but in fact have to go back
to Nitori to purchase specific ones that fit the fixture in my
apartment.

Of course.

I returned home with some string and some pins and spent
the evening hanging photos of all my loved ones around the
borders of my bedroom by the light of my laptop, with a can
of Sake and music blaring. Nesting day one: complete.

The next day I scouted out the local area and picked up a
few bits from the supermarket including a box of fancy
cakes as a gift for my next-door neighbour/landlord. I was
taught that introductions were important in Japan, and that
bringing a small offering was a nice way of setting a good
tone within the community. I was feeling pretty nervous and
had my introduction speech prepared:

Hello, my name is Ashley, please call me Ash. I'm from the
UK, I am here to teach English in a high school. I have a
present for you, nice to meet you...

Very basic, but also extremely daunting as I was about to
use it on a real human who understood the words I had been
practising.

Standing at his door I noticed the sense of grandeur; he had a special door with ornate wrought-iron knots to suggest he was the leader of this complex. He also owned an electronic doorbell with a camera fitted into the mechanism. Noticing all this, my heart began to beat harder. This guy must be of some importance in the neighbourhood. I was sure he would be nice. I pushed the bell.

I could see shadows moving about inside through the frosted glass; they came closer and disappeared until finally the door opened a tiny crack and I was met with a low grunt and an inaudible but recognisable, "何?" (Nani? — What?). Ok so this was going well so far.

I saw before me an elderly man wearing tracksuit bottoms and a yellowing white baggy t-shirt. He was barefoot with flip flops and his posture was hunched somewhat. His grey stubble and balding head told me he didn't take care much of his appearance, and the way he looked at me told me he was not a man to mess with. His eyes were dark and hollow and he did not care to be disturbed. A musty odour of damp and tobacco emitted from the crack in the door.

My fight or flight instincts were kicking in; my head was screaming fight whilst my body was edging away slightly. I decided the former was the best option and here is what transpired:

[NB the whole conversation consisted of him using very old and informal Japanese and me using my basic broken Japanese.]

"Sorry to bother you, I'm your new neighbour," I began.

"What do you want?!" he said with a rough tone.

"I have a present for you… nice to meet you," I said, bowing as low as I could. "…Err…err… my name is Ash." Another low bow. "I'm from the UK. I am an English teacher …" I bowed once more.

"What?" he repeated.

"I have a present for you… here you are."

I handed the bag over to him and the door opened a bit further as he peered into the contents below.

"What is it?" he asked.

"It's cake… here you are… please take it."

He reluctantly took the bag.

"Do you know about the trash?" he said in a gruff tone.

"Can you repeat that please?" I asked.

He mumbled something inaudible.

"Sorry I only speak a little Japanese, could you say it once more please?" I asked again.

"TRASH!!" he shouted.

"Err…. Ok, thank you," I said, bowing for the final time.

The door closed and I heard the lock turn.

"Well I think that went pretty well," I uttered to myself as I quickly retreated inside my own place, covered in sweat, trembling and confused. What an unpleasant man.

The word 何 took on a new meaning for me that day. He said it with such passion and distaste. He was not a man who enjoyed human contact or any sort of social interactions as I came to discover over the next few months.

After my first encounter with my cheery next-door neighbour/landlord, I went down to the trash collection area to vet it out and figure out why he felt so strongly about it. I found the little concreted area filled with baskets of various colours and a large sign with a list of items acceptable for disposal. I recognised the days of the week so figured out the trash was collected on both Mondays and Thursdays. As for what they collected and how I deposited it there was anyone's guess, so I took a picture and went back upstairs to translate it.

Eventually I asked a Japanese friend to kindly translate it for me as my dictionary wasn't a lot of help. It turned out that there were thirteen types of garbage and each had to be disposed of in a specific way. Apparently Warabi was known for its strict waste disposal rules.

A couple of weeks later I returned home to find a mysterious wooden block hanging on my door with 木当番 and 月当番 written on either side. The first thing to come to mind was the Plagues of Egypt or The Scarlet Letter. Somehow, I had been selected and branded with an unknown curse or warning. Had the mafia been notified of my whereabouts and was I now being hazed?

On further inspection, I realised that the symbols referred to Monday and Thursday respectively which could only mean one thing. Trash day. I sent a picture to my trusty Japanese comrade who said the symbols meant "your turn", but what event I'd been nominated for I was none the wiser. After deliberating for a while my friend suggested I returned next door to ask my old buddy. She kindly offered to translate over the phone for which I was eternally grateful.

I begrudgingly traipsed next door and rang the all-seeing doorbell. As expected I was greeted with his ever so friendly catchphrase: "NANI?!" and I instantly passed over the phone, asking him to please speak to my friend. I waited anxiously as they spoke, and it sounded like she caught him out a few times. He returned the phone to me, forced a slight bow and closed the door.

Stunned, I asked my friend to explain what had just transpired. She explained that the wooden sign was to notify me that it was my turn to overturn the baskets the trash went into. I was to then pass it onto the next person and it would rotate itself throughout the entire building every few months or so. I asked her why he seemed taken aback halfway through the phone call, and she relayed that she had told him to be politer, to slow down when he spoke to me and to stop using Japanese slang.

She said that my Japanese wasn't too bad and if he only complied to these basic instructions, I would be able to understand him. She said he was terribly rude even in Japanese and apologised that I had such an awful landlord and neighbour. At least it wasn't anything personal.

This encounter then sparked a round of complaints which resulted in a multitude of phone calls from the apartment management company to the real estate agent, and onto me. I would receive nonstop calls whilst at work and would have to excuse myself to answer them. I was told that somebody had made a formal complaint to the management company about 'someone' not putting out the correct trash on the correct day and that 'someone' had been leaving their window permanently open, allowing the rain to get in.

At first, I thanked them for the notice and thought nothing of it, but after the fourth call I started to take it personally. I asked them if they were just calling me or if they were calling everyone in the building.

They struggled to answer and I took that to mean they were only calling me. I asked them who had made the complaint and they told me the caller wished to remain anonymous. I asked how the caller knew specifically that it was me putting out the wrong trash on the wrong day. Was I being followed and monitored?

I also informed them that I didn't actually own any windows that opened outwardly. I had only two sliding doors at the back of my balcony which no-one could see, because I was on the top floor at the back of the building. I also only had a tiny window in my kitchen that leaned backwards a crack acting as a vent. So, this caller, whomever they may be, was deeply misinformed.

They apologised and told me they would call everybody else in the building. A week went by and yet another call came through. I was told that they were sure I was the culprit and I informed them that I was deeply upset and offended.

I had spoken to the landlord personally and he had explained to my friend about the trash collection and how it works. My friend had also translated the whole rule book into English for me so I couldn't have been trying any harder. I was so careful to take note of what everyone else had put out on trash day to ensure I was laying down the same items.

Another few weeks went by and one morning, while I was putting my trash in the collection area, I noticed my plastic PET bottles looked differently to everyone else's. The others were clear whilst mine still had the labels and bottle caps on. Could this be my error? Surely not. I asked a colleague at work that morning and was informed that the bottle label and caps were made of a different kind of plastic and must be removed before throwing out.

So, after this whole debacle, it turned out that I was in fact the notorious trash fiend, and had somehow offended an entire building enough to make multiple complaints to the management company who then had to contact the real estate agent in order to contact me and relay said complaints.

Oops. My bad!

During the initial six months in my apartment, I was very careful with what I purchased because I wasn't sure how long I would remain in Japan, or if my job would employ me for a second year. I only allowed myself to buy the bare necessities: pots, pans, a table and single chair and bed from IKEA. I had to settle on a single bed due to room size restraints, but managed to find one with a socket in the headboard to charge my phone so decided that was a fair compromise.

I made the trip back to Nitori shortly after the first trip to purchase the special light bulbs. I took a picture of the strange fitting in my ceiling to be sure, and showed it to the shop assistant who then showed me the very expensive only option available. I reluctantly accepted and paid the ¥4500 (£30) for each bulb (needing three for my main rooms).

Returning home to fit them, I realised that the ceilings were too high to reach, so had to venture back out to the supermarket to get a small footstool. Finally, I proudly connected the huge bulbs that cost more than a weekly food shop and ceremoniously turned on the first one in the bedroom.

Lovely. We had light.

I quickly fitted the second one and thought I'd better check that it worked after all the hassle. The only problem was I couldn't locate the light switch anywhere. Scanning the room like a moron, I simply couldn't detect where on earth the switch was. How was I to use my new investment?

I sent over a message to the real estate agent on the emergency group chat they had added me to, and asked if I was missing something. They replied saying that I should have a switch, to which I replied with a negative. They contacted the landlord back and forth over the course of two weeks, who eventually informed them that because that room in question was a Japanese style room with tatami mats, they thought it was best to include Japanese style lighting too. This therefore meant that I had to once more return to Nitori to purchase yet another light but this time an even more expensive one with either a cord attached or a remote control to turn it on and off.

I was so frustrated and thus commenced the five month long "Dark Protest of 2016"; the most stubborn endeavour of my entire adult life.

I refused on principle to waste any more money on a light

for a room that was essentially a glorified closet, especially as I couldn't return the already opened useless bulb. I purchased a torch instead.

Jumping forward briefly to early January 2017, I decided that I would finally give in and make my place into a home and not worry about what I purchased and how I would have to dispose of it at the end of my stay there. I realised that I needed to start living for the now and not the future, so I had a splurge day trip to IKEA.

I purchased a sofa bed, coffee table, bookcase and the pièce de résistance, a brand new, big, white, shiny, corded light for my living room. I returned home to set up my new baby with anticipation.

Stepping down off my stool with fingers crossed, I pulled the chord and YATTA! We truly did have light!! I was overcome with the weirdest sense of pride, accomplishment and warmth, for this was not just any old corded light.

To me it was what the light represented: the end of a five-month stubborn protest where I had not necessarily felt happy or at home. Now I was settled after deciding to re-contract for a second year.

"ただいま!" (Tadaima!) I exclaimed out loud and proud to myself. It's a term that means: "I'm home!" It was only at this point in time where I felt like I finally had a home to call my own. It was a nice feeling, and one that changed my outlook on things for a while. It truly signified the start of my life in Japan.

One day during the following week, I was running late after work and had to go home to change before rushing back out to meet some friends. I dove straight in the shower as soon as I returned home, and halfway through, heard the doorbell chime a couple of times.

I was expecting a parcel so threw on some shorts lying on the bathroom floor and ran to the door without a top on. Answering the door, I instantly recognised my error when I was greeted with a high-pitched banshee scream. As my brain retuned to its normal frequency, I realised that the banshee was in fact a young woman. She covered her eyes and I told her to please wait.

"Was I truly that hideous?" I laughed to myself.

I returned fully clothed and apologised; explaining that I had been in the shower. She introduced herself as my next-door neighbour from the other side. She was bringing me a bag of mikans (Japanese oranges) as a traditional New Year's gift. I introduced myself and apologised once more before she bowed and retreated into her apartment.

So that was now two neighbours who loved me.

6

TADAIMA PART THREE

ただいま#3

Community

After a full season of living in my new apartment and establishing a daily routine, I was walking to the station one morning, when I got to thinking about what a wonderful neighbourhood I had landed myself in.

Neighbourhoods bring about comfort, community and curiosity, and that is exactly what I grew to love and embrace during my stay in my apartment.

As for the location, I had all the amenities I could have ever asked for within a five-minute walk; two combinis, three supermarkets, two huge department stores, the post office headquarters (open until 7pm compared with 5pm everywhere else), the police station headquarters, hospital, hairdressers, parks, temples, and so much more.

The locals were all very friendly, patient with the language barrier and extremely helpful. The ladies at the supermarket recognised my face and would stop for a chat about the mackerel bento box I always bought (one lady spent half an hour explaining Japanese fabric softener to me the first time I purchased some), the young guy who owned the local bike repair shop bowed his head each day, and I looked forward to my monthly hair cut at the barbers where I could practice my basic Japanese on the friendly staff who knew my usual style by heart.

I come from a small town in Suffolk, East England, and Warabi isn't far off the same sense of homeliness. I am quite a curious individual and would often go on lengthy walks to explore my surroundings and in doing so discovered many temples, shrines, parks and a Pizza Hut that delivered (useful for dinner parties).

There were many map notice boards dotted around pointing out all the local points of interests, one of which I followed only to find an abundance of old and traditional buildings and family-run shops. As I've already said, I am quite the avid Pokémon Go player and one day, whilst walking around on one of my many explorations, I decided to use the in-game map to find new locations. To my surprise it worked. I discovered a large and open family park, complete with a hidden forest trail where local kids would leap over the stepping stones rising out of a running brook. Just around the corner, I noted the tall wooden posts synonymous with a family grave peering out over a wall, and upon closer inspection was blown away by the grandeur of a great Buddhist Temple complete with a three-tiered pagoda, all completely hidden by the neighbouring houses.

I appreciate community and that's exactly what Warabi was. I saw the same children each morning walking to school clutching their many bags adorned with even more bags hanging from them, with keyrings galore attached to everything in their possession. Some brave individuals would smile as they passed, some just stared in awe and most ignored my existence completely, bashing into me as they passed as if I wasn't even there.

I observed the same commuters each morning who gave a slight nod or entertained me without knowing it. Seeing them each day allowed me to create whole lives for them in my head and imagine what kind of individual they were.

There was the young woman with the green dolly shoes and matching green bag. I always recognised her by her 'Japanese run' - the kind of run that gives the impression of rushing when in reality it is nothing more than a fast walk, with her feet moving at half the distance but double the speed.

She both irritated and amused me every time I saw her. I would think to myself, "If you only left five minutes earlier each morning, you wouldn't have this issue." I imagined she had two young children who refused to get out of bed which added to her tardiness. She was too nice to shout at her kids or scold them, permitting them to run the household.

I would overtake, only for her to run and catch up moments later. She would speed ahead only for me to overtake in turn. This pattern of insanity repeated itself the entire way to the station where I would find myself powerwalking to win the imaginary race. I, of course remained victorious each time and offered a celebratory smirk as she arrived on the platform. I am pretty sure she had no idea this silent marathon occurred each morning.

Then there was the guy who worked in the retirement home next to my apartment. He was quite the portly individual and was forever running late for work (a common theme). He had long thick hair and wore big over-the-ear headphones that held his fringe in place across his damp forehead.

Every time I saw him, there would be beads of sweat falling from his brow onto his face. He definitely stayed up late each night playing online community games, chatting to cyber friends all over the world. His alarm never went off because he forgot to charge his phone on a regular basis and just caught the train late each morning. Clearly time management is a difficult skill to grasp for many morning commuters.

I have always been criticised by my ability to powerwalk everywhere. When I was younger my sister would often tell me that I looked like an idiot as I glided along the path, weaving in and out of the crowds at lightning speed. It has become my natural walking speed and I am therefore never late. It is very rare for me to encounter another individual who embraces the same 'talent'. That is until I came to Japan.

While most people in Warabi went about their day at a snail's pace, there was one girl around my age who, if I left my apartment five minutes later than usual, I would encounter. Her sense of fashion was a tad racy for Japan and she was met with many stares from onlookers regardless of her speed.

She often wore extremely high heeled shoes, with short shorts and long fishnet tights. She carried a large backpack in the shape of a games console with many keyrings hanging from it. She too was an avid powerwalker and my inner obsessive-compulsiveness could not help but silently challenge her each time we met. It became a race to each set of traffic lights.

Unlike the previous contender, she was an enthusiastic rival and our winning streak stood at fifty-fifty each way. Occasionally our eyes would meet if we both stopped at the same set of lights and we knew it was game on. I couldn't help but let her win in my head due to the insane height of her shoes. I could never have maintained such composure whilst wearing those things.

She was walking to a job where people didn't appreciate her and where she could wear whatever she wanted. That, or her boss was not strong enough to manage a team and they walked all over him; wearing and doing exactly what they wished. I imagined her in some avant-garde coffee 'slash' shop. Not slash in the sense of blood and murder, but those new hipster mixed coffee shops that all compete for your attention.

During my time in Tokyo, they seemed to be popping up all over Harajuku and Omotesandō, and I managed to visit flower-coffee, book-coffee, pet-coffee, bike-coffee, clothes-coffee, gallery-coffee, home-coffee, even sticker-coffee shops. I imagined her working in a too-cool-for-school, edgy rock-coffee shop that put more emphasis on concept than product quality.

At the halfway mark from mine to the train station, I reached my favourite part of the route: a little winding manmade stream etched into the rocks with an old water pump at one end. Flowers and cherry blossom trees lined the path and kids often caught tadpoles in the stream and played in the reservoir at the end. At regular intervals along this route, the morning run of mothers stood with their 'lollipop lady' flags, allowing the school kids safe passage across the roads. Each morning I felt a little sense of reward as they would nod to me in greeting as if I'd done a good job crossing the road unaccompanied.

At each end of the stream stood a Kappa statue. Kappa are demons or imps found primarily in Japanese folklore. The statues are used to warn children not to play in or near bodies of water as Kappa have been said to lure and pull people in. I often witnessed an old man who brought daily flower offerings to the statue on his way to the station. I think this is such a sweet gesture; I loved the way people and nature work almost in unison in Japan.

And finally, we come to the happiest man in the world…
well to me he was anyway. As I approached the station
some mornings, I was greeted by an elderly man whose job
was to greet people and wish them a happy morning. He
was always positioned by the bus station and was, without
fail, clad in a tailored suit, sometimes wearing a bright
orange jacket on colder days. He had very neatly cut
greying hair and his eyebrows stretched high into his
forehead making his eyes appear wider and thinner. He
wore the biggest grin I'd ever seen and all this,
accompanied with his deep and low bow, made me feel
content and at ease each time I saw him.

Oftentimes, I wished I could express eloquently enough
how much he cheered me up each morning and would have
loved to have wished him a happy day too. One summer's
day, walking to the station, I saw him riding a bicycle with
two bright flags sticking out of the back, waving to passers-
by and shouting good morning to them. He was like a little
morning greeting faery, spreading the morning joy to all the
miserable and half-asleep commuters.

I liked to imagine he was a retired youth worker or carer
and wanted nothing more than to wish people well. He
would wake up every morning with a smile and performed
at least five selfless acts each day. He would return home to
his wife, who is an avid gardener, and greet her with a warm
cup of tea and a kiss. He would see his children and
grandkids at the weekends and spend all his time whittling

them toys out of wood. He was skilled at origami and wouldn't dream of saying no to anything or anyone.

This is what I liked to imagine. It (regretfully) transpired, however, that he was nothing more than a local politician who stood there each day asking for people's vote!

I'm sure he was a lovely gentleman, but probably didn't have the time to commit to all the categories I placed him into. Sometimes walking about aimlessly ignorant of the truth is far superior in my opinion than the bleakness that comes from the reality.

I loved watching the elderly walking and chatting away to their old and greying dogs. One lady would drag along an old red wagon for her Beagle to clamber into when his feeble legs had enough. Others carried water bottles to spray on walls or trees each time their dogs cocked their legs. One woman carried huge BBQ tongs to pick up all matter left behind by her dog. Then there was the man with the gorgeous Golden Retriever who thoroughly enjoyed his post-walk bath outside their front door. I liked how each person went about their day unabashed, without worry or fear of judgement from onlookers.

Occasionally, I did actually require urgent assistance, like the time I was taken ill during my first winter. The pharmacy around the corner from my apartment went above and beyond to help me in my hour of need and without being asked to, printed off an English diagnosis and instructions on how to use each medication provided. This

53

was the side of Japan that visitors rarely hear about because it's so unheard of in our own societies.

Besides my landlord and the mikan lady from the other side, I shared my little cul-de-sac with many other residents, some of whom I rarely saw and others I was on a greeting only basis with. There was the tiny old woman who lived opposite me. She lived in a small house that reminded me of the house from the Disney movie Up. I liked to think that it was the first house to be built on this block and gradually all the other apartment buildings were erected all around it. She used to sit on her wooden balcony and look over the paddy fields in the summer heat, enjoying the sound of cicadas chirping away in the breeze.

During my stay there, I would often step out of my front door to see her handing out her sundries in her nightgown. I imagined she was about five foot three but appeared to be much smaller due to her arching posture. Her spine mimicked a curve one could only achieve with the use of a compass. She was graced with a single arm and on warm days would don her formal attire, accompanied by a prosthetic arm and white gloves, whilst during the long chore-filled afternoons she would potter about the neighbourhood unashamed by her uniqueness. She very sweetly greeted me each morning or gave me a wave if I had my headphones on. I wholeheartedly had her to thank for making me feel completely welcome in this neighbourhood.

On the ground floor of my apartment building lived a young

family by whom I was regularly knocked back each morning as I descended the stairs. Their front door would burst open with a loud bang, and a stampede of children poured out to play with their Anpanman bikes and toy cars. They were so fearless, always shouting "KONNICHIWA!" whenever they saw me. When do we lose this sense of innocence and lack of judgement that is so rare and important in today's world?

The final person I'm going to mention is a woman who lived not in the same building as me, but at the end of the tiny cul-de-sac. Her place stood next to a miniscule alleyway that created a small opening for residents to leave and enter the road. I had been using this route for quite a while, until one evening when everything changed.

I was running home one evening during Warabi's local festival, seeing the incredible firework display growing evermore impressive in the distance. I thought if I could climb up onto my balcony, I would have the perfect view all to myself and my two friends who were visiting from England at the time. I ran on ahead to open up the doors and used the alleyway as always.

All through the streets, residents and neighbours alike had left their houses to join in on the festivities and were now watching the display. As I approached the alley, I was stopped abruptly by a short woman in her fifties. She shouted "SUMIMASEN" (excuse me) at me which surprised me into pausing. I halted and the altercation that occurred (all in Japanese) was as follows:

55

"EXCUSE ME! YOU!" she proclaimed.

"Yes? Sorry, good evening" I offered.

"YOU CAN'T COME THIS WAY!" she shouted into my face.

"Excuse me?" I asked, a little shocked.

"YOU CAN'T WALK THIS WAY!! LOOK AT THE SIGN! CAN YOU NOT READ??" Her tone was getting worse.

She directed me to a portable fence with a paper sign on it, which I read every time I used the walkway. It simply stated that this route was for residents of this area only.

"Oh yes, I know. I understand. I live just there," I said, pointing to my apartment.

"YOU DON'T LIVE HERE! THIS IS FOR RESIDENTS ONLY! READ THE SIGN!" Her accusatory tone was getting hasher by the minute.

"I am a resident. My apartment is that one just there. I walk through here every day," I said pointing to my apartment once more.

"YOU DON'T LIVE HERE!" she exclaimed.

"Ok, sorry, goodbye…" And I just walked away because I was so mad at her blatant rudeness and audacity.

She didn't like that so she followed and stood in front of me, blocking the way.

"DO YOU UNDERSTAND? DO YOU UNDERSTAND?!" she said in the most patronising and abrupt way.

"YES, I UNDERSTAND. I CAN READ!" I shouted back at her.

"YOU CANNOT WALK THIS WAY!" she shouted once more.

I yelled something like "WHATEVER!" in English and walked away. By this point my friends had caught up and I heard her announce, as clear as day, in Japanese, "OH GREAT, MORE FOREIGNERS!"

I grabbed my friends, telling them to ignore her, and in doing so, recalled the word for 'rude' in Japanese and shouted it back at her.

What a truly horrific woman! She was clearly one of those neighbourhood watch types who had nothing better to do than stand at the entrance of 'her' alley and punish those for daring to enter like the trolls depicted in old folk tales. She didn't like that I lived there and, quite obviously, didn't like the fact that I wasn't Japanese.

I understand and appreciate the older generation's sometimes radical views upon people of other cultures living in their community, but I kept to myself and didn't bother anyone. This attack really upset me and made me feel even more like an outsider than I already felt. I didn't feel welcome in that moment and it put a downer on the whole evening.

To be the bigger man, I never used that alley ever again, and spent the remainder of my time in Japan walking around through the road, in the hopes of avoiding her or the memory of her.

At the end of each day, I took the same route home on my evening commute. I did not see or notice the same people but appreciated the same vibe and feeling of completion of each day. The guy in the bike shop would be wheeling the bicycles inside, the morning dogs would be having their evening walks, and the smell of dinner emanated from house to house so much that I would think of those cartoon characters from my youth levitating and carrying themselves through the air towards a windowsill pie.

As the sun set and the evening curfew jingle played once more (a pleasant-sounding alarm used to notify the kids that it was time to go home. Its true purpose was to test the public loud speakers in each area that are often used to notify residents of any emergencies of public concern such as earthquakes or tsunamis, but it had adopted this dual use, killing two birds with one stone), neon lights and lanterns came to life, the sound of cicadas began to die down throughout the summer, and in the winter, kids and adults retreated inside houses behind condensation-rich windows that emitted steam when opened.

I felt welcome (as a whole), accepted and relaxed in this community; I followed the rules, kept to myself and was left to my own devices. I would say that after the amount of time I lived there, the small cons were massively outweighed by the vast pros. I felt like a member of this community and despite living alone, never truly felt alone. Warabi had all that I could ask for, and I know that my experience in Japan would have be completely different were it not for this small but crazy mini society.

7

TRAIN CHRONICLES #3

電車物語#3

New Attraction

The brain is a mysterious and wonderful organ, and one thing I absolutely love and hate about it is how in times of intense stress or fear, thousands of thoughts can whizz through your synapses in the matter of a single second.

This entire anecdote I'm about to divulge took place in no longer than fifteen seconds, but at the time felt like much longer.

I was standing on the train one morning looking out the window with my back to the other passengers. It was a particularly busy morning so I liked to pretend nobody else was there by distracting myself with the views of houses and mountains in the distance passing by.

My phone buzzed in my pocket with a notification from a friend. They had sent me a link to a compilation video of funny pugs, so I put my headphones on and fired it up. There is something about animal videos that allows me to lose myself for hours, and I still had fifteen minutes left so I indulged myself.

Chuckling silently to myself and fully imagining life with my future pug, I was all of a sudden abruptly jerked backwards and found myself being dragged halfway out of the train. I began thrashing around for dear life, trying to grab onto anything I could - handrails, doors, another person's leg, while all the time trying to work out why some unseen force had decided to eject me from the carriage.

My mind began to race a mile a minute:

"Am I being attacked? Is it because I was laughing to myself? Was I being too loud? Was there an evacuation announcement? Did I miss it because of the pugs? Cornelius is a good name for a pug. They're like squishy little aliens. Is there an invasion of some sort? Don't drop your phone! It'll cost a fortune to get it fixed. Can you imagine the faff of getting a new phone sorted in Tokyo? My back is going to hurt if I land awkwardly. I wonder if I'll get the day off work…"

When I finally managed to turn around I was faced with the culprit: an elderly woman who was laughing hysterically. This was not what I had expected to find. Why was she laughing? Did she see the pug videos over my shoulder too?

I followed her eyes to the source of the laughter and noticed she was trying to unhook her bag from mine. I was wearing my rucksack and somehow as she brushed past me to leave the train, the zip on her handbag became entangled in mine and we were now one.

The station chime announcing the door closing began to sound and we both locked eyes, knowing we had a matter of seconds to disconnect. As if contacted telepathically, four new strangers jumped in on the action and were assisting in the great untangle of zips.

I still had my headphones on at that point and could hear a mix of muffled Japanese and the sweet snorting of pugs. I thought I had better say something to diffuse any possible tension so I apologised. The woman looked shocked, maybe because I spoke Japanese or maybe because it was the first time I had spoken up. She said it was ok and that the whole situation was hilarious.

As I already mentioned, it is against the rules of Japanese train etiquette to talk loudly so when a foreigner begins shouting apologies (I didn't realise the volume of my voice until I pushed my headphones down to my neck) at a hysterical elderly woman, it is bound to attract some kind of attention. I looked around and saw that we had every eye on board directed towards us.

Thankfully, we managed to split just seconds before the doors closed and by this point passengers had realised what was happening and were smiling and laughing in unison. I bid my temporary Siamese twin goodbye with a hearty bow and smile, and the gesture was returned in earnest.

I waved her off as the train roared to life once more and

rotated back towards the window to return to the
pugs. Never a dull moment on these morning commutes.

8

NATSUKASHII

懐かしい

As I continued to explore Tokyo during those first few months, one concept that became ever clearer to me was that of embracing your inner child well into adulthood. I would observe grown businessmen walking down the streets carrying mobile phones clad with fluffy keychains or bags covered in a multitude of badges depicting their favourite anime characters.

I visited comic book stores full to the brim with mature audiences lined with bowing heads engrossed in this month's latest issue, and game arcades that were open until the early hours of the morning allowing street fighters and taiko drummers that extra inch of practice time.

Arcades in Japan were like nothing else on Earth. They were an amalgamation of lights, sounds, shininess and all things cute and fluffy. They were a safe haven that rejected judgement, and visitors could happily and comfortably embrace their guilty pleasures at will. Most arcades had six to ten floors and it seemed that the higher you go, the more extreme the players become. Usually the first few floors were full of crane machines of various kinds and these were pretty tame. Unlike in the west, most of them did involve some sort of skill as opposed to luck.

Around the 4th or 5th floor was where the magic started. Players there honed in on their craft and I would often see men and women smashing their high scores on dance machines, or on hand-eye coordination-based musical games that required you to hit buttons in a futuristic whack-a-mole style. It was so much fun to just stand and observe customers going to town on these machines and it was often prohibited to take pictures of them.

The top floors were usually set in the dark and the air was thick with smoke from all the gamblers that sat there for hours on end surrounded by pots of change and empty cans of coffee.

The most impressive sight was of those using the piano-like games where players must hit the matching keys to the moving lights on the screen that move in time with the music. Players would bring their own white gloves that enabled them the ability to move at the speed of light. They must have practised daily and moved using muscle memory rather than actually following their eyes because no human alive could coordinate that skilfully!

This innocence so quickly lost in the west is carried beyond adolescence in the east, where everything from air conditioning units to loaves of bread has a mascot character attached to it. I would always hunt to find the cute face on each type of food in the supermarket or bakery which somehow worked in making me want to buy the item even more! It worked because there appeared to be less concern from onlookers, allowing the masses to proudly purchase and own whatever they found attractive in the moment.

I was instantaneously sucked into the first wave of Pokémania when I was a child. I was an avid Pokémon trading card collector and the games appealed to me as if they were a real-life counterpart. I soon outgrew this fad, but then the next wave of collectable items swarmed the UK. I would purchase the latest Pokémon game on handheld console every other year or so, but moving to Japan in the year of its 20th anniversary ignited a strong sensation of nostalgia within me. It allowed me to unlock that juvenile sense of perspective I lost so many years ago.

I visited the famous Mega Pokémon Centre in Ikebukuro soon after arriving and was blown away to discover the company had rereleased the original card set from my childhood to celebrate their 20th anniversary. The inner collector and obsessive-compulsive child inside of me saw no other option but to complete this set.

"Challenge accepted," I thought, and suddenly found myself getting excited opening packs of cards designed for Japanese children. On the third pack opening, I pulled the infamous Charizard card. THE card. The card that was dubbed the most expensive and highly sought-after card ever and that once upon a time had sparked many fights on the school playground.

I specifically remember my dad getting into a fight with another kid's dad over this card on my behalf. As I held this revamped celebrity in my hand, a Japanese man walked by, sighed at me and said in the calmest voice "Ahh… natsukashii!"

The Japanese have this ability to sum up an entire situation in one simple yet effective expression. In this case, that is natsukashii. I wish we had an English counterpart. 'Nostalgic' somehow doesn't quite do it justice in my opinion.

Back in the shop I noticed a poster advertising two promotional cards from my childhood to those who traded in any old cards. If you handed over twenty old cards, you would be gifted with either a promo Pikachu or a promo Charizard card (two mascots from the franchise). I had just purchased a few packs so thought why not buy a few more, trade in forty cards that I don't want then I can add both of these special cards to my new 'mature' collection.

I happily strolled up to the counter to claim my prize when the woman manning the station looked at me with a melancholic expression and regretfully announced that the cards I was offering her were not acceptable. The only cards eligible were those from the 90's and 00's.

Part of me began to channel the child version of me when I would lose a coin toss in a trade with my friends. As I glumly begun to walk away, a man in the queue behind stopped me, opened up a box full of old cards, counted out forty and casually handed them to me.

At first, I refused to accept them but when he insisted wholeheartedly I eventually gave in and accepted his offering. I passed them to the lady and was rewarded with the two limited edition cards.

The entire exchange happened so quickly that I didn't have time to process what had taken place. I bowed multiple times to the man and used all the polite and grateful Japanese I could muster before eventually walking away.

What a completely altruistic and selfless act from one kind and unassuming gentleman to another on the natsukashii trip of a lifetime. From the looks of it he was an avid collector, but there was something about the way he looked at me for a split second as he handed over those cards. It was that of a child giving another his last sweet in the playground. Although he may hurt, he knew it would be unequivocally appreciated and treasured.

I did in fact continue to collect this particular set until near completion due to many factors: it fuelled my inner compulsion, it fed my inner child's search for that natsukashii feeling, and quite frankly it was a hell of a lot of fun! Every now and then I would visit the centre or look at this collection and it would make me smile to remember this day and the exchanges that took place amongst the hustle and bustle of this hectic biome.

Around the same time, I had a particularly interesting event unfold around the new global phenomenon that was Pokémon Go.

If you were living under a rock during 2016 and you missed it, Pokémon Go is an augmented reality mobile game that uses GPS in order to catch digital monsters in real life locations. The tagline, "Gotta Catch 'Em All" entices players to explore their local towns and cities in order to locate each of the (originally released) 151 Pokémon.

The game releases the pocket monsters in waves, keeping the anticipation and excitement high when new rare creatures would drop and spawn in the wild.

Seeing that everyone kept to themselves on the trains gave me ample opportunity to scout out my competition, learning what level each player was at, and how many characters they had caught. Of course, in true Japan-fashion, the art of go-big-or-go-home stood strong with mobile gaming, as I noticed (by secretly peering over their shoulders) that just one month after the game's initial launch, many players were already halfway to maxing out their experience levels and owned multiple versions of the rarest Pokémon released thus far.

"How do these people possibly find the time to play in such a hardcore manner with full-time jobs and families? What is their secret?" I thought. Well, as it turned out, it was all down to another tricky little mobile app.

During the early stages of the game, certain cluster spawns of select Pokémon would appear in specific areas for extended periods of time (known as nests). App developers created user-collaborative tracing applications whereby users could input current and live updates of the aforementioned nests. This, of course spread like wildfire and created a ripple effect through the streets of Tokyo.

I would often be going about my own business, uninterrupted by anything or anyone, when suddenly I would stumble upon a huge gathering of people collected outside a McDonald's restaurant or by temple gates, all tapping away at their phones frantically. The joy and excitement this game gave me, and the interactions with others it would bring, encouraged me to get out more and wander around on my days off.

After work and during weekends, I explored Tokyo every free moment I had, finding new and exciting places to visit. One place that soon became an all-time favourite is the man-made district of Odaiba. The journey to Odaiba was a unique experience in itself, riding the monorail over the Rainbow Bridge that stretches out across the Tokyo Bay. It made me think of a futuristic rollercoaster as it spirals around the supportive columns towering out of the sea, and hurtles downwards towards the skyscrapers and iconic Fuji TV dome, all the while gliding silently over the golden beach and bustling streets below.

Odaiba is amazing, and that is all there is to it. It's a bizarre little place that somehow amalgamates the past and the future.

As I stepped off the monorail, I arrived on a wooden boardwalk that offered one of the best views of the Tokyo skyline. Complete with a Statue of Liberty replica, I would stand and take in all of the most impressive landmarks in one frame. The Tokyo Tower, Skytree, the Metropolitan Government Building and the Rainbow Bridge, all reflected in the sparkling bay below.

I often walked along the beach to look out over the water, and it soon became one of my safe spots; those places that are special and unique to you. Spaces that bring forth a sense of relaxation and contentment. Sitting on the warm sand, enjoying the cool breeze and taking in the perfect reflections of the boats and wooden posts rising out of the sea, gave me time to truly soak in my new surroundings and savour my new life.

Oftentimes during a busy working week, it was very easy to forget both my successes and how lucky I was. Moving to Japan had been a lifetime goal of mine, and Odaiba gave me the time and space to ensure I never took this for granted. If I ever felt myself ignoring my surroundings, I scheduled in a Saturday trip to my new thinking spot to refresh my brain. This all proved too much one day, however, when I became swept up in a globally publicised scandal.

It was a Saturday afternoon, the sun was high and warm, the air the perfect temperature. I sat on the edge of the shore watching a group of elderly women force their perfectly groomed miniature poodles into a photo shoot, all positioned together atop large rocks resting on the water's edge.

The crowds were not as heavy as I came to expect from a weekend visit to Odaiba, and my thoughts turned to the small lines at the ice cream stand. Thinking of which flavour I should buy, I found myself being jolted back into reality as a young girl jumped over my legs and ran along the beach. I watched her playing in the sand for a second until I felt a sharp rush of air from behind me as a young man followed suit, running towards the girl. He was followed by an older couple and another young girl.

"They must be together," I thought, as they were heading in the same direction. But then they tapered off in separate directions. Something felt amiss.

Hearing sounds of excitement coming from the opposite direction, I turned to see if they were being followed. The scene I was faced with can only be described as a human tidal wave.

Still sitting by the water's edge, perfectly still like a rabbit in the headlights, I was jolted back to reality suddenly and I knew I had to act fast.

I jumped up and began to sprint at full speed, intertwining between the fleeing masses towards higher ground. I was now part of the stampede.

In full panic mode, I looked around frantically at the people running around me and realised they didn't seem as concerned as I was. In fact, they seemed to be laughing. This was no laughing matter! Didn't they understand the severity of the situation? This was no time for jollity.

Turning to the young woman running to my right, I asked in a breathless panic, "Where are we going?"

"ラプラス！" (LAPRAS!) she screamed in my face.

I must have misheard. My confused brain was hearing names of cartoon characters.

"Sorry, where is everyone going?" I asked once more, opting for a more formal Japanese.

"ラプラス！" (LAPRAS!) she repeated in an excited manner. "OVER THERE!" she continued, pointing out across the water.

At once it dawned on me. We, and by we I mean, tens of thousands of Japanese people and a very confused Englishman, were not running for their lives against the full force of Mother Nature. We were in fact running to catch a digital, albeit extremely rare, Pokémon.

"Well I haven't caught this one yet, so I better get a move on!" I thought as I overtook an elderly man and leapt over a fallen child.

Twenty minutes of running later, I found myself standing on a tiny concaved island connected to the mainland, surrounded by excited individuals rejoicing in their latest catch. I joined in with the gathering masses as I added this rarity to my collection.

Looking out over the bay as I made my way back towards the beach, I could see a dark shadow of people in the distance, sauntering its way ever closer like a fierce storm cloud waiting to erupt.

Later on that evening, a news article appeared on my phone of police arriving at the scene of a Japanese riot. This riot turned out to be a chaotic gathering of people playing Pokémon Go. In Odaiba. My stampede made the news.

The police were forced to act as crowd control because people were running in front of cars and ignoring the traffic signals, all with the single aim of getting to the coveted Lapras prize.

It transpired that this Pokémon was being released twice a day in specific areas across Japan. Gamers had used the tracing Apps to locate the secret areas, word spread like wildfire and the stampedes ensued. Unbeknownst to me, I just so happened to be caught off-guard in the epicentre of it all.

Stories like this are just one of the many reasons why I absolutely adore this country. This kind of mass hysteria could only occur here. Where else would you encounter such a large gathering of people running as one to find a digital creature? Where else would you encounter this kind of crowd full of positive and supportive individuals?

There was literally a surprise waiting for me around every corner. I never knew what to expect and there was always something weird and wonderful waiting to be discovered.

From here onwards, I would look back on this day as a light reminder to fully embrace my inner child and to not worry too much about upholding a mature and professional demeanour.

When I first discovered that these people from all walks of life were running like madmen along the beach to catch a single Pokémon, I entered full Pokémon Trainer mode and strived to "be the very best, like no one ever was!"

I galloped onwards with gay abandon, leaping over fallen children to achieve my goal with pride and triumph. From here onwards, I refused to allow myself to feel shame or embarrassment for becoming excited about things deemed culturally inappropriate for adults.

If I wanted to buy a giant mochi-mochi Oddish plush and display it proudly as a house plant, then that is what I would do. If I wanted to visit the Studio Ghibli museum and play on the life-sized Cat Bus, then I would ensure to ride that bus with full gusto; and if I wanted to run at full force through the crowded streets of Tokyo to catch the latest wave of Pokémon released to the world, then I would run like I was being chased by a mass murderer and embrace my inner Ash Ketchum, shouting "Get!" (ゲット！) as I claimed my next digital comrade.

However homogenous Tokyo and its inhabitants may have seemed, there were still so many pockets of niche and wonderfully diverse individuals just like this within each sector, all seeking the same thing: something to captivate them, appeal to their senses and ultimately make them happy.

I added these encounters to my Journal of Firsts. The first time I embraced my inner child unfeigned, the first time a selfless act of kindness was inflicted upon me in my new home, and the first time I ran for my life from a fake tsunami and towards a new chapter of my life.

9

MENDOUKUSAI

めんどうくさい

As I settled into my new life in Japan, I was keen to practise my Japanese as much as possible, and yet even though I was living in the city with the highest population of Japanese people on the planet, I was struggling to find opportune moments to use the language.

I had studied Japanese for several years at high school and had reached a basic understanding of the language to the level of a native kindergartener. Having not practised for almost ten years, I picked up some private lessons for a year before moving to Japan, so my level was at a more introductory conversational level.

If I ever asked an expat living in Japan of their level of Japanese conversation skills, I would naturally hear a collection of mixed responses, but one commonality for those living in the larger cities was that they struggled to find opportune moments to use this complex new language. Why was this, you may ask... well, put simply, because the locals wished to practise and hone on their own Eikaiwa (English conversation) skills.

There was a sense of distaste from expats towards using English when conversing with Japanese natives, and I would enter lengthy debates on the topic whenever in the company of other expats living in Japan. I would hear streams of people exclaiming, "They gave me an English menu!", "I spoke to them in Japanese and they responded in English!", "They only approached me to practise their English!" as if it was some great injustice. But the thing was – Japanese natives wanted to learn, they wanted to converse with us expats informally. So what should it matter? Well, I guess the answer is – it depends.

I encountered these situations on a weekly basis, and whilst it concerned me early on, that concern soon dissipated. I owed this to an expression introduced to me whilst explaining my situation in a slightly over-emotional way to a colleague one evening. This expression is known locally as 'mendoukusai'. It literally translates to 'bothersome', 'troublesome', or even just plain 'annoying'.

I would frequently hear this word thrown around at times of trivial crisis. Maybe someone had dropped an ice cream on the floor or maybe someone was one yen short of the perfect change to purchase something. Maybe someone had parted their disposable chopsticks poorly, creating a harsh array of splinters, or perhaps I would be at the front of a long line of people waiting to go through the station ticket gates and my IC card had run out of credit. Naturally one could have attached 'shouganai' to many of these situations but in that bothersome moment the word 'mendoukusai' fit perfectly.

I was subjected to many awkwardly fascinating encounters in the vast mega city and had quickly learned how to gauge people's intentions. For the most part they had harmless and selfless agendas; they just wanted to chat. And, ok, sometimes I would have to stand there for a few uncomfortable moments as I was told, "You are very skilled at using chopsticks!" or, "I know a man called John in Yorkshire, do you know him?" or even, "You look like Zac Efron, can I take your picture?" but did this kind of interaction really take away anything from my life? Did it perhaps add something to someone else's existence? Perhaps. I had simply learned to entertain the idea that each interaction was both significant and insignificant in its own respect.

One such encounter occurred during Tokyo's first November snow in fifty years in the winter of 2016. I was given the day off work and I took it upon myself to pursue some city office-based necessities. On my way home through the back streets of my ward I stopped to pick up a handful of snow that lay upon someone's garden wall. In doing so, I was observed by an elderly gentleman on a bicycle who stopped to tell me in English that what I was holding was in fact snow. Now this conversation could have gone one of two ways.

1. I could have simply ignored or brushed him off as

      I've witnessed so many people doing in similar
      situations;

2.   I could have responded and humoured the guy,
      discovering the intended route of conversion.

I took the latter and am so grateful for doing so, for it was one of the most weird and wonderful conversations I had partaken in during my stay there. It transpired that he visited England many years ago. He could only remember a few interesting words from his time there, which he then practised on me. Said words included: 'large', 'breakfast' and 'rain'. He was very proud to use them after so many years and was delighted to converse with an English native.

His phone suddenly appeared and without warning I was standing there in the cold watching a slideshow of images depicting his six pet cats. The look of adoration and tenderness on his face as he explained each cat's story was quite humbling. I understood only the gist of what he was saying but I felt he was happy to just have some company on a cold and wintry day.

Our journey ended at his front gate where a couple of his cats came to greet us vocally. I was invited in for some green tea to which I kindly declined. He shook my hand, thanked me and told me I had permission to always talk to his cats whenever I saw them.

Now how 'mendoukusai' was that? A kind-spirited, cat-loving, elderly man simply wishing for a moment of my attention to discuss snow and cats, allowing us both to go about our day completely unscathed and distracted from any intercultural stigma or ignorance.

I regaled my friends with an account of my morning to receive a multitude of responses. Some claimed they would have taken option 2 as I did, but most revealed they would have in fact followed route 1, missing this surprisingly uncanny exchange of minds on a rare November snowy afternoon. Which would you have taken?

If I gleaned anything from this conversation, it is that I am glad I entertained the thought of stepping out of the shallow mindset of some, and partook in some genuinely interesting and thought-provoking conversation. Using two broken languages to discuss a man's true love for his animal companions, we both walked away learning a little about the other's culture (and I can't deny the free listening and speaking practice was a treat on my part). But all jokes aside, from then onwards, I took any opportunity I could to appreciate these moments because I never truly know where the juncture will lead me.

A similar but less genuine incident used to present itself at work from time to time in the form of the wood shop teacher. I never actually learned his name but gave him the moniker of Mr Noble for reasons which will soon become apparent.

A short, bespectacled, elderly man whose appearance remarkably matched that of Hayao Miyazaki appeared one day at the back of the staff room. We were informed he was the new part-time wood shop teacher. He kept mostly to himself, whittling by the printer, and would occasionally stroll up and down the room, slowing each time he passed the 'foreigner's' table. In his head, he thought his actions most inconspicuous but in reality, he may as well have held a flashing sign reading, "I WANT TO SPEAK ENGLISH!"

He would stop each of us every time we picked up handouts from the printer and would regale us with facts about our native countries. My co-workers would be stopped in their tracks for ten minutes at a time, getting trapped in his web of awkward conversation. I managed to avoid such contact for a couple of weeks by using the printer in another room, until one day when I was cornered in the toilet.

I was washing my hands when I felt the presence of somebody standing behind me. Turning slowly around, I was shocked to find him standing directly behind me.

"You are from England!" he announced.

"Err, yes, I am. I'm Ash. Nice to meet you."

"Queen Elizabeth! She is suspicious…"

"Oh … erm…" I wasn't sure how to respond to this comment.

"Ah, mistake. Your queen is very… NOBLE!" he explained.

"Thank you?" I was now very confused.

"Ah, THE BEATLES! YELLOW SUBMARINE!" he continued. "Very good music. They are famous. ABBA, Dancing Queen. I like Dancing Queen. Kylie Minogue. She is very sexy. My wife is not sexy. English girls are sexy. English people like Kylie Minogue!"

I couldn't bring myself to correct his geographical errors or sexist remarks.

This encounter left me confused, amused, bemused and… used? I could tell he had been wanting to tell me this for a while due to the speed in which he vomited all this information on me the second I turned around. The whole conversation left me stunned for words, especially at the location and the way the situation presented itself. I thought about my snowy friend from before and felt the intentions were of a very different nature. I couldn't help walking away feeling like an English conduit, rather than the recipient of a warm and meaningful conversation.

This scenario was not a one-off and each time I found myself in an enclosed space with Mr Noble, he would continue to regale me with facts about my own country, however fictitious. Once he had his way with me, he would halt all conversation, allowing me to leave or he himself would walk away. I was his English tête-à-tête bitch and this had to end.

This was mendoukusai. There is a culture of reading the air

83

in Japan; assessing the situation and acting accordingly. Mr Noble was not capable of doing this and would catch me and the four other foreign teachers off guard whenever opportunity presented itself. His intentions were extremely obvious and these gatherings soon ceased when he left the school for good, leaving nothing but strange and confusing memories.

Unfortunately, this type of discussion was more prevalent than the former. I would still engage in as many conversations as possible, the only difference being that I was able to understand the intent much sooner rather than later, allowing me to swerve away from the one-sided and into a beneficial encounter for both parties. Sometimes it could be difficult and things could take a very awkward turn into solely a teacher-student role. It was these kinds of encounters that myself and many foreign residents would try to avoid or extinguish.

I always aimed to be polite and imagine if the roles were reversed. I would think to myself, 'Would I attempt to practise Japanese with a native in the UK?' I honestly don't think I would for fear of embarrassment on both parts or becoming a burden.

One exception occurred at Taronga Zoo in Sydney in 2013. A group of Japanese students were buying kangaroo toys in the gift shop and the shop assistant was asking them about donating to a gift aid. Panic ensued as the tourists didn't understand what had been said. The woman tried to tell them many times and, in the end, I whispered behind them in Japanese what had been said. They all bowed and thanked me with great appreciation; in fact, they waited outside the shop in order to take a photo with me. I felt this situation was worth breaking my own rule to help them out and make them feel at ease.

I feel there is no right or wrong answer to this topic. I believe ignorance and expectation are the wrong approach because it creates judgement and destroys open-mindedness, but if each scenario is addressed independently, I may be pleasantly surprised and leave gleaning something new. That or I'll leave with a fun conversation piece for my next dinner party.

10

TRAIN CHRONICLES #4

電車物語#4

Rejection

On most train carriages, at each end, there are rows of priority seats. One rule for the use of this area was for people who have injuries, diseases or heart problems.

Boarding the train one day after a stressful day at work, I noticed that all seats were occupied bar four out of the six in the priority area. One of which was taken by a young man, and the other an elderly woman sitting next to him. The man was sleeping and rocking side to side, occasionally knocking into the woman. I assumed they were sitting together.

At the next station, as the train drew in, the man jolted awake, noted his location and left the train promptly. There were now five empty seats in the priority zone. Usually, I would stand in this area, but on occasion would sit until a worthy customer stepped on, to whom I would gladly donate my seat.

After the busy day I had just endured, I sank deep into the empty chair next to the woman, turned up my music and zoned out.

A couple of seconds went by and I was abruptly brought back to reality through the means of a few sharp jabs in the right arm. I jumped and turned to find the elderly lady shouting something at me in muffled Japanese.

'Could she hear the music through my headphones?' I wondered. 'Is she asking me to turn it down? Was the conductor announcing something of importance over the tannoy?'

I pulled off my headphones to hear the end of her rant, and asked her to repeat herself. She showed me the badge attached to her coat lapel, it had a white background with a picture of a heart on it. She had a heart condition, and was seated in the correct place. Duly noted.

I looked at her, not fully understanding why she had caught my attention, and excused myself before attempting to pull my headphones back on. I was graced with yet another few pokes in the side. What was this woman after?

She seemed disgruntled at something I was doing, and again pointed to her badge and gestured to the priority zone: she did not think me worthy of this area. I hadn't earned the right to be seated here. I told her there were four empty chairs, so my presence wasn't too disruptive to the Feng Shui of the carriage. Not only that, but just seconds before, a young man was sitting in the exact seat I now found myself in. Was she saving this seat for somebody else? Did I smell?

She shouted something incomprehensible at me yet again, and to avoid any future confrontation and through fear of upsetting her heart badge any further, I stood up and walked to stand by the door.

After the day I'd had, I was not in the mood for a train-based altercation and instead settled at glaring at the woman to notify her of my angst. I left the train at my station a few stops later and that was that. Just a disgruntled, self-entitled woman, claiming her territory. I wouldn't let it ruin my day, so purchased a milkshake on the walk home. Problem resolved.

The following day, I regaled my friends with the story of what had happened, and it turned out there was a pretty valid reason as to why she persisted in poking me.

Use of the priority zone was not the sole rule regarding heart conditions. Passengers were encouraged to turn off their phones and transmitting devices whilst occupying this area for fear of interference to pacemakers from electronic waves. It wasn't me she had been upset with, it was my phone. Now I felt like an idiot.

Personally, I couldn't see how moving two feet away would

make any difference as there were many people in the vicinity using their phones at will, but I should have been more aware and respected her wishes, because once again, Japan and its rules-that-make-sense-but-don't-completely-make-sense took centre stage.

11

ODAIJI NI

お大事に

I've been visiting Japan since I was fifteen years old, and each time I return am still nowhere closer to understanding the mystery surrounding the iconic 'face mask'. Everywhere I went, crowds of people lined the streets wearing surgical masks, mimicking some eclectic flash mob.

During my childhood, said masks symbolised sterile environments or bacteria-ridden procedures. My evil orthodontist or the nurse who froze the wart off my knee as a kid wore this type of personal protective equipment.

In later years, I would come to work in a Veterinary clinic and nurses and vets alike would wear these masks in theatre or during certain dangerous procedures. I would strap a mask to my face during quarantine events such as kennel cough or when dealing with young unvaccinated patients. These masks served a purpose under dire and life altering circumstances. So why do people in Japan wear them as casually as wearing a pair of glasses?

My teachers and superiors in the UK, when asked about this odd phenomenon, would explain that residents of Japan were afraid of pollution and radiation caused by smog, power plants and any other carcinogenic chemicals drifting through the streets of the over-populated country.

Each time I visited Japan I would secretly try to investigate the truth behind the mystery, never actually asking individuals for fear of accidentally offending somebody. After moving to Japan, I would still wonder what secrets could lie behind the marvel, until one day I was asked to wear one myself...

Tokyo was extremely cold in the winter and the combination of a lack of central heating and double-glazed windows brewed up a nasty recipe for a festive illness, especially when mixed together and cooked for twenty minutes each morning during the commute to work. Trains became breeding grounds for newly discovered bacteria and suddenly I felt fortunate that humans lacked the ability to see the particles spewing out of each individual standing at close range to each other in those sardine tins on tracks.

Spring came and went, and all was well until the arrival of summer when people began to sweat as they marched to the station at full speed so as to not miss their train. The conductors were yet to realise that the heat of the morning, coupled with the added body heat from each passenger, equated to an equally disgusting mix of fluids as those encountered during the winter.

This time around, commuters were wiping beads of cascading sweat with hands, towels or whatever they could locate, all the while holding onto any surface they could to support themselves in the rocking carriages. It was especially fun when I had to physically peel myself from a neighbouring passenger in order to alight the train, leaving with someone else's juices along my arm.

Inevitably, during my first winter in Japan, I succumbed to my first 'Japanese cold' and was sent to the nurse's office where they decided to send me home for fear of infecting other colleagues or students. Influenza was taken very seriously, and a simple diagnosis was enough to give you a few days off work. Before setting off, the nurse told me to seek further medical assistance and to purchase some masks so as not to infect other people around me.

'HALLELUJAH!' I thought. The Holy Grail of information had finally been revealed to me during the one time I lacked the energy or enthusiasm to celebrate after many years of shortcomings.

"Odaiji ni," she shouted at me as I left the office. What a serendipitous expression this turned out to be. I turned to my dictionary as I glumly walked away and upon discovery, felt suddenly uplifted as such a powerful new phrase was added to my repertoire. The term means to wish someone well, to take care when sick, or to get well soon. Perhaps it was my state of delirium, but this simple phrase seemed to add some sort of substance to the situation; making me feel a tad better if only for a moment.

On the way home, I stopped by my local pharmacy to pick up some medication and my first ever mask. Weirdly excited, I found the mask section (yes there was an entire section) and was blown away by the multitude on offer. The woman behind the counter sensed my confusion and came over to help. Explaining that I was sick and this was my first time purchasing a mask, she recommended the best model accordingly. She passed me a packet labelled M size, and I explained as best as I could that my head is quite the vast globe to which she chuckled and swapped it for the XL size.

I paid the woman and she asked if I needed help putting on the mask to which I nodded solemnly. She smiled and carefully opened the packet, pulling out a thinner packet containing a mask which was then opened, revealing the white goods inside. She hinted for me to remove the mask myself and acted with her hands how to open it up.

She mimed for me to place it over my nose, pinch the bit of metal inside and pull down the concertina of fabric on each side to fit accordingly over one's muzzle; not forgetting to place the straps comfortably behind my ears. It fit perfectly and at once I felt like I should be in some kind of apocalyptic video game, shooting zombies and rabid dogs as I make my way through an abandoned hospital.

"Odaiji ni," she announced as she beckoned me out of the store. I was once again struck by this magical new phrase.

As I walked home I felt as if everyone's eyes were on me until I noticed that in fact nobody even batted an eyelid.

The next day, on the train commute to work, I wore my new comrade and was gobsmacked to discover that, whilst without previously wearing a mask people would glare at me for coughing or sniffling, today with a mask securely protecting other passengers from my germs, nobody even acknowledged my existence. I was like a mucous-ridden Harry Potter under my cloak of invisibility; impenetrable to diseases and bacterium of all kinds.

As each day went by, I would walk to the station bare-faced, soaking in all that well-required Vitamin D before retrieving my protective shield from my bag and placing it over my face as the train rolled into the platform. This would come to be a staple part of my daily routine for the remainder of my time in Japan.

Whether or not it actually protected me from the masses crammed into each carriage, each person coughing, sniffling, sneezing and just generally breathing in my direction, or whether in fact it held some kind of placebo effect was difficult to tell, but I did not experience any illness-related symptoms after investing in those little white cloths of grandeur.

I later visited a friend's house for a dinner party and as one of the guests walked in wearing a white mask, another offered a kind "Odaiji ni," to which the reply given surprised me profoundly.

"Oh, I'm just wearing this for fashion…"

Mind. Blown.

Years of wondering, months of clarity and suddenly in an instance, one second of pure pandemonium.

So, it transpired that people could in fact wear these garments as fashion accessories.

I have since witnessed individuals wearing masks of all shapes and colours (the black ones that young guys wear actually looked pretty awesome). I've seen elderly citizens pad theirs out with extra cotton wool or with customised knitted covers.

The vice principal at my school would often wear one due to hay fever, claiming that it protected him from the high pollen count. I was even told by a student that wearing a mask helped to keep her skin moist and free of blemishes as she would not be subjecting it to the harsh elements. Some students even wore them as a security blanket; feeling more confident with their face securely hidden behind a barrier of judgement from the world.

So, I guess, there you have it; there is no right or wrong answer to this occurrence, it just is what it is: a culturally acceptable notion as common as wearing a pair of glasses or a woolly hat. Whether or not the wearer is sick or simply wants to protect their face from harsh UV rays, the mask will sit as a constant reminder of the time I learned a new useful and significant phrase that for a split second made me forget my troubles and crack a cheeky smile.

12
TADAIMA PART FOUR

ただいま#4

Best Week

Occasionally, the vast multitude of people I
encountered each morning began to wear thin, and I found
myself becoming somewhat irritable at the lack of personal
space, especially as the majority of those people did not pay
attention to their surroundings. I observed people walking
into bins, posts, walls and other people more than often.
This was only exacerbated when mobile phones, umbrellas
or bicycles were added into the mix, not to mention a person
riding a bicycle, holding an umbrella and playing on their
phone all at the same time. This fanciful delight was
exactly what I encountered one fateful morning on the way
to work.

It was a cold Friday morning in November; the skies were
grey, the wind howled and the rain poured, mimicking the
perfect typhoon. In other words: the perfect British
summer's day. Cold and miserable, I left my apartment a
bit earlier than usual because rain often meant busier trains.
The whole week had not been a fun one, and my mind was

racing as I walked through each day's festivities, allowing me time to process and wind down before the last day of the week.

On the Monday, I was forced to scold a student quite badly in class for mimicking me and not paying attention. I still felt guilty about it as this was the first time I had to raise my voice whilst teaching. I wasn't yet used to playing the bad cop and remembering the girls face as I shouted at her made me feel like I could have reacted in a more professional and constructive fashion.

Tuesday, I had a difficult meeting with my supervisor which didn't go as expected. We had discussed a few ongoing issues with some of my classes and the discussion took an unexpectedly heated turn. It ended on a positive note, but it was a huge learning curve on my part.

Wednesday was full of a bad run of classes, which happens on occasion, but was exacerbated by the already negatively trending week.

On Thursday, I was returning from the lunchroom and tripped and fell whilst walking up the stairs. I could be quite clumsy when ascending stairs and had been known to fall on many occasions, but as I looked around to see if the coast was clear, I saw a student just below laughing in hysterics at me. As I tried to brush it off and make for a smooth recovery, I slipped once more and twisted my back which was difficult to conceal as I let out a tiny but audible whimper. The student was then concerned and I spent the next five minutes persuading her not to run for the school nurse.

Which now brings to me Friday, which was about to trump the entire week. I had just reached the halfway mark to the station, back still aching from the fall (at what age do we go from 'Ash fell over today' to 'Ash had a fall today'?) and happy for the cursed week to be over. As I rounded a corner in one of the smaller backstreets, I noticed a cyclist heading towards me. The young man, dressed in his black suit, was holding an umbrella in one hand and using his mobile phone with the other.

At this point of the journey, there weren't any pavements so I moved swiftly towards the opposite side of the road, allowing him plenty of space to pass. Some unseen force then decided to step in because the cyclist had changed directions and was now (seemingly) unintentionally heading directly towards me. I was standing right up against a wall and had nowhere else to relocate to. My options were limited so I braced myself for impact; holding out my hands in front to hopefully take some of the blow.

Unbelievably, he was completely oblivious and forced his front wheel straight through my legs, as my hands reached out and pushed his handlebars away. Unfortunately, the force and speed at which he rode bent my hands back and sent me flying.

I was knocked off my feet and landed flat on my back in a puddle of water. The impact knocked the wind out of me, forcing my umbrella out of my grasp and throwing it somewhere overhead. At first, I laid there stunned by the fact that I had actually been knocked over by a bicycle of all things, then I remembered the week I had just been glad to end, and was overcome with anger and frustration.

The bicycle owner stood over me and peered down as my face was flooded with negative emotions. Unable to read and assess traffic safety, he clearly read the message written all across my face, as he steadied himself, and shouted "GOMENASAI!" (sorry) in my direction, before returning his feet to the peddles and riding off at full speed.

OK. Wow. I was now a victim of a full-on hit and run, albeit from a pedestrian on a bicycle. Other pedestrians had now stopped all around and were stood staring, but nobody came to check if I was ok. In truth, I was in a lot of pain and, with an already tense back, found it difficult to roll over. My backpack, which had somewhat cushioned the fall, made steadying myself awkward, and with passers-by watching me, I flailed about in the middle of the road impersonating an overturned tortoise.

My hand located my fallen umbrella and I used it to pull myself onto my feet. I attempted to wipe myself down but by this point my clothes were already soaked through with the muddy rainwater, so I hobbled to the station, using my umbrella as a walking stick.

Arriving at work looking dishevelled with stains all over my shirt, I explained what had happened to the boss and he sent me to the nurse's office at once for some pain relief. Our school nurse was a lovely, short, rotund lady who didn't speak any English, but had the most nurturing demeanour about her. I tried to explain in Japanese what had happened, but somehow all the useful vocabulary had momentarily left my brain. Not caring that I'd look even crazier, I renamed one of my hands 'Ash' and the other 'Mr Bike', and acted out the whole scenario to the nurse's enjoyment.

She understood at once, and ran over to see if I needed holding up. I changed into the indoor slippers provided, and she led me over to a hospital bed where she asked me to take off my shirt. She stuck a heated gel pack to my back and explained that I would need to wear it for 24 hours. The relief was instant and I took a few spares to put over the rest of my back.

So, this concluded my best week. I'm sure there was some form of karma, wisdom or lesson I was supposed to glean from this experience. Whether it was to be more patient with students, to tread more carefully when climbing stairs or to wear a helmet with flashing lights to deter cyclists, I would prefer it to come in a form that didn't result in me laying in a puddle of mud for all my neighbours to see.

13
TRAIN CHRONICLES #5

電車物語#5

New Beginnings

Mondays. Everyone's favourite day of the week. The freedom of the weekend is over, and the harsh reality of everyday life resumes its nasty work. Drones of citizens collate in unison, joining the snake-like commuter traffic, as they prepare for the launch of a new working week. In essence, Mondays suck.

I have never been part of the I-hate-Mondays-club, as previous jobs required either early or late shift work, but working in Tokyo and seeing how people operated (or failed to), opened my eyes to the sensation.

Walking to the train station one Monday morning, I noticed more intensely how people were bumbling along with their morning coffee, some moving at a trot as they were inevitably running late. The caffeine had obviously not yet kicked in for the morning as people from all angles were bumping into me like naked mole-rats going about their business in the burrow.

Arriving at the station, I was overcome by the sight of throngs of commuters, reminiscent of a scene from The Walking Dead. It was now a dog-eat-dog rush to the platform where even more lines of people stood patiently awaiting the slow approach of the train, also running at full capacity.

The doors opened and this is where the magic happened. Japanese people had somehow adopted octopus-like powers and could now manipulate their bodies in a way unseen in the western world. Personal space was eradicated and what would have once been deemed inappropriate in both societal standards and under health and safety regulations, had become a challenge of how many people could fit in one vehicle.

With each passing station, passengers left and were replaced tenfold, only intensifying this human game of Tetris. Certain carriages were naturally busier than others purely because most commuters would suss out which doors opened by the stairs at their destined station, limiting the walking time and distance at the other end.

The trains were most likely to be running a little late due to 'passenger injury' and it was common for station officials to hand out excuse notices for those arriving late. Schools postponed their first-class period and shortened the length of the morning classes to cater for the late trains. I was not used to how reliant people were on the rail system before

103

coming to Japan, especially coming from a country where most people drive and are in charge of their own punctuality. I would predict the traffic and leave earlier to ensure I never arrived late.

It was a strange phenomenon that I would soon become accustomed to over the years. I used to try leaving earlier on a Monday morning, but it actually intensified, the earlier I set off. I soon began to leave a bit later, making a world of difference in terms of the mass of people on board, still arriving at work before the allotted time expected of me.

One thing I took from the Monday commute, however, was the art of suffering in silence. Despite the delays, number of passengers in the station, on the platform and in the trains themselves, I almost never heard any complaints of any kind. People would wait patiently, occupying themselves with a book, newspaper or games console, until it was their turn to move an inch or two forward on this inevitably trialling and cyclical journey to work.

It is one more thing the western world could take note of. The timeless expression 'Patience is a virtue' comes to mind.

14
KI WO TSUKETE

気をつけて

My Journal of Firsts took a whole new direction at the beginning of 2017 during a Winter trip to Sapporo. Myself and three friends I had made during the initial orientation training weekend upon arriving in Japan, reunited for a skiing adventure.

We were the only four British citizens in our programme so naturally we struck up a close bond from the get-go. I shared a room with two guys, Owen and Nico, both of whom I shared a similar sense of humour and was instantly drawn towards their confidence and brazen outlook on life. Hannah was our lively and outgoing Scottish comrade that made up the fourth member of our team.

We explored Tokyo's night scene together all fresh-eyed and bushy-tailed from our long flights across the globe. We exchanged information and decided to stay in touch; planning on reuniting as soon as we could. Nico was to be relocated to the island of Okinawa, Owen to Osaka and Hannah to Ehime on the island of Shikoku.

Our reunion trip got off to a rocky start when we discovered at the airport after all the hugs and excitement that our flights had been cancelled due to heavy snowfall.

At the check-in counter, we explained that we would instead catch the Shinkansen (bullet train) up north, and the woman merely looked at us and uttered a worrying "Ki wo tsukete". I ignored this new phrase at first in my stage of mixed emotions. Our flights had just been cancelled, yet we were reeling at the impending adventure into the unknown.

After a brief stay at my place for the night, we arrived at Tokyo station to board the first shinkansen up to Sapporo. We were issued with non-reserved tickets as it was pretty last minute, and all the seats were taken. We had two options: stand in the aisles, or find somewhere to sit on the floor.

We found a large foyer section in the first carriage by the toilets, so set up camp there for the approaching long journey ahead. After about twenty minutes or so, the ticket man walked past and informed us that we were in the first-class carriage and had to move. Begrudgingly, we collected our belongings together and walked through the next few carriages to find a new spot to rest.

Conditions were much more cramped and there was barely anywhere to sit. By the first-class toilets we had enough leg room to sit stretched out and then some, but the spot we eventually chose to rest could only just about cater for the four of us sitting crossed-legged. We made do though, as we ate our snacks and played games; all the while the train roaring through the Japanese countryside, forcing its way ever northwards in the cold, harsh winter's morning.

Five hours later we left the safety of our doorway nest and were forced to transfer trains somewhere near Aomori, in the north of Honshu. Disembarking the train, we entered a small local station and could sense at once the pure chaos that awaited us. Obviously, many other people were trying to reach Sapporo and had the same idea as us. There were now hundreds of passengers crammed on the snow-covered single platform awaiting the next train, and the situation was only getting worse as more people poured through the ticket gates.

We could see on the notice board that there were only a couple of trains running that day and they were a few hours apart. We needed to get this next train.

As it finally pulled into the platform, we relocated to stand by one of the incoming doors. Shivering, we waited for passengers to exit the train but no one did; the entire train was full and not a single person was getting off.

The four of us tried to link arms whilst holding onto our luggage as a stampede of people were suddenly attempting to force their way through a single doorway. Myself and Nico made it safely onto the train but Hannah and Owen were disconnected from us and pushed out of the way, falling out of line.

Meanwhile, onboard, Nico and I were being shoved further

into the carriage with no possible way out. If the other two couldn't get on, we would be separated for the remainder of our journey.

Frantic, I could see through the window the mad rush of people becoming more and more frustrated as they pushed with all their body weight towards the door. This was carnage. I turned for a brief second and somehow out of the corner of my eye spotted Hannah standing by the carriage toilets. Thank goodness, she had made it. Three down, one to go.

A group of young women all travelling together had also made it onto the carriage and decided they wouldn't allow anybody else through, as they were now satisfied with their own situation and anybody else would ruin their vibe.

Outside the windows, I could hear the faint sound of the chime signifying the closing doors. Looking over at Hannah, we could see the worried look across her face, telling us there was no hope for Owen fighting his way out on the icy platform.

The doors closed and the train began to rumble its way back to life. Passengers outside looked tired and disappointed as they were ushered away from the train. They would have to huddle together on the platform, or seek warmth elsewhere for a few hours as they awaited the next train.

Now wasn't the time to rejoice, for our group had faced one casualty. Poor Owen would be making his own way to

Sapporo. We tried and we fought, and we failed.

Or so we thought.

Struggling to locate Owen outside the window to let him know we would wait for him at the next stop, I looked through the carriage towards Hannah, and could see a beaming grin forming across her face. As if by magic, there was Owen, reaching up from the corner of the foyer, waving in our direction. Somehow, he had made it on the train too, but something was wrong.

He was wedged up against the wall by the masses of passengers and nobody was letting him move. Hannah tried to ask the group of women to move as they were now occupying a large area with plenty of space for the remaining passengers to move into.

I could hear her asking them politely to move but they were ignoring her. She persisted to nudge them slightly out of the way to no avail, and others around them began to notice what was happening.

Then, like a phoenix rising out of the ashes, Owen, now exhausted from the previous battlefield, stood up to his full 6ft 1" height, loomed over everybody else on the carriage with the last of his energy, and announced very clearly with his resonating voice, two words: "MOU CHOTTO!" (meaning 'a little more', but in the context meant move out of the way).

Suddenly, many things happened at once: all eyes were on him, the gaggle of women jumped and parted like a 90s boyband hair style, a mosh pit of arms appeared and both Hannah and Owen's suitcases were being air lifted towards Nico and I in the centre of the carriage, followed by Hannah and Owen themselves.

At last, we had made it and were safely reunited. Now was the time to rejoice. We exchanged awkward hugs in our cramped space, all the while the entire carriage of passengers were staring in our direction and the group of women were still standing, shocked and confused by what had just taken place.

With each passing station, somehow more people boarded until there was zero space to sit on the floor, rotate, or even move. After a couple of hours, the four of us took it in turns to slide down onto the floor as oxygen levels were depleting, and without food or water, we were beginning to feel faint and exhausted. The train was continuously delayed even further, and we ended up standing for a total of five hours.

After a total of ten hours, we finally arrived at our destination to find the roads covered in twelve-inch-thick sheets of ice and pavement labyrinths dug out of six-foot snow drifts. As we braced the treacherous roads, seeing many pedestrians slip and slide, one unfortunate man fell, hitting the back of his head with a loud thud.

People rushed to the scene and as he stood, he was

overcome with a chorus of "Aahh, ki wo tsukete!" This phrase materialised once more... but what did it mean? I attempted a quick Google but was unlucky at catching the correct pronunciation so was unable to search for it sufficiently.

The next day, a few hours north of Sapporo, I stood on top of a mountain in Asahikawa. We had decided to check out the scenery and I was attempting (and failing) the fine art of skiing for the first time. Having taught me the very basics of the sport, my friends and I decided to ride the gondola to the top and glide our way down the easier route pathed out. I had sufficiently grasped the concept of moving, turning and stopping, and was gaining confidence with each descent. After a few successful runs, we decided to tackle a route on the next level of difficulty, but still within the easy range.

Halfway down the slope, I lost traction and took quite a hefty fall; twisting my knee and landing in a tangled mass of body parts face down in the snow. It transpired that we had taken the wrong path when reaching a fork in the route, and the terrain became much steeper than we expected.

As people slowed down to pass, a sense of déjà vu overcame me as that new danger-related phrase appeared once more. It transpired that 'ki wo tsukete' was used to simply wish that the receiver takes care of themselves. Standing on what felt like the top of all creation, overcome with fear, 'take care' was the last thing I needed to hear, but some part deep inside of me appreciated the intent and in some way, it helped ease my primitive fear… momentarily.

Paralysed with fear for the first time in my adult life, I physically couldn't move a muscle, let alone glide elegantly down the side of a mountain. Hannah and Nico were far ahead and were probably at the bottom by now, but Owen, Mr 'Mou Chotto', was by my side. His calm demeanour and gentle take on the situation encouraged me to make my way down the mountain at my own pace. I didn't feel at all confident in my ability to ski any further, and the only thing I wanted was to get off this slope.

Realistically I knew that my only option was to continue down, for I could never safely make my way back up the path to ride the gondola back down, but my flight senses were kicking in and I was ready to give up.

Passers-by continued to offer their vocal support along with a very patient and empathetic Owen ever-present by my side, and it was due to this encouragement that I did not succumb to the elements and made it back to the base safely. It (only) took an hour and the sun was beginning to set on the horizon, so the group decided to take one last ride to the top for a go on one of the more advanced routes. I stayed at the bottom to recover and reflect upon my traumatic, albeit educational, experience.

Despite being absolutely terrified from my fall, I felt completely at ease with these three people I had only really met once. Our bonds were tight and we looked out for one another. We were all in the same boat and I knew that judgement was a nonissue here. I was able to be myself wholeheartedly around this group and allowed myself to embrace each new experience as it presented itself. Each of us had a skillset that the others didn't have and our daily routines and ease about how we functioned together were evidence of that.

A week later I had regained my confidence with skiing and the trip ended on a high as I departed from Sapporo, gracefully retiring from the sport, and having learned a new useful Japanese staple phrase. After an emotional goodbye at the airport, the four of us returned to our cities of residence and our lives returned to normality. We would continue to stay in touch and reminisce regularly of this amazing winter adventure.

The winter holidays came to an abrupt close, and my daily routine thawed from hibernation, which meant it was time to return to work.

A few days into the new semester, I experienced a horrifically shocking encounter on my morning commute, where I would for the first time use my new phrase instinctively.

It was a Tuesday morning, and I entered a trance-like state, autopilot mode, taking my regular route to the station and boarding carriage number one, knowing that it would stop right at the stairs at my final stop. The carriage wasn't overly crowded but was busy enough that passengers were forced to stand.

I perceived a me-shaped empty spot in the middle of the walkway so took post there in between two Japanese men. I noticed the man to my left was dressed rather distinctively compared to all us other professional drones in black suits. He was sporting a floor-length white trench coat that made me ponder what secrets hid beneath, a large white brimmed hat with a black sash around the middle and a black polo necked woolly jumper that almost hid a barely exposed tattoo creeping up the side of his neck. This was a first. Tattoos were extremely rare in Japan.

I tried to imagine him in a modern-day western movie, fearful of dirt spoiling his clinically clean attire, and chuckled out loud to myself. The stray grey hairs on the side of his head gave the impression that he was perhaps in his forties but his face told me otherwise. He had a baby face but the glazed-over tension behind his eyes alerted my flight instincts and unexpectedly I was reminded of that same innate fear I suffered high up the snowy mountain. My mind often runs away with wild ideas so I shrugged off this unwarranted reaction at once.

One stop went by and I knew I would be on this train for six more so placed my bag between my legs and held onto the hand rings, always secretly wishing to swing like a gladiator down the carriage every time. Holding onto the ring next to me, the dapper man raised his head sharply to look me square in the eyes.

In the realms of wolves, he would have howled or cocked

his leg, claiming his territory and enforcing his alpha status, but by this point, more passengers had boarded and the environment had become much more intimate; reducing any free space around me. I avoided eye contact the same way I would when walking amongst the herd of sheep living next to my childhood home in order to avoid freaking them out, thinking this would calm him likewise. Unfortunately, my ovine husbandry did nothing of the sorts.

The train roared to life once more and another stop went by when quite abruptly the conductor exercised the emergency breaks, jolting each passenger somewhat in the process. In all the commotion, my bag resting between my legs fell slightly and gently brushed against my new friend's right leg. I bent low to reposition it, offering a "Sumimasen" to the leg owner as I straightened up. In place of a nod of acknowledgement, or expression of gratitude, stood a face filled with the level of rage only ever witnessed in Spanish bull fighting arenas.

I tried to ignore the situation, putting it down to a bad morning or perhaps he had skipped his morning coffee. Another station went by and I could still feel those red eyes fixed upon the side of my face until the train came to a complete stop as his journey ended. Many passengers left the carriage at this popular stop and my new-found associate would soon follow suit, but not before elbowing me directly on the side of the head as he turned around, half knocking my glasses off in the process.

This was the moment I chose to use my new phrase,

thinking it would defuse the tension and add light to the clearly accidental act. "Ki wo tsukete," I said with a smile, and what happened next shocked both me and the entire carriage of people.

The man's elbow continued to rest against the side of my head, and in an instant, I found myself seized by the shoulders and neck, and propelled against the train door with a most aggressively modern cowboy screaming clearly in my face, "GAIJIN!!" (a derogatory term for 'Foreigner'), before rotating and swiftly exiting the train.

The entire time I was frozen in a state of complete shock with so many questions racing through my mind: 'Why are my glasses still hanging at a funny angle? What made this cowboy so angry all of a sudden? Why is he so offended at my foreign status? I'm a resident here, fool! Someone just stood on my bag. What secrets do you have under that coat?'

Nobody came to my aid, if anything I felt suddenly penalised for the whole debacle as current passengers moved away from me, continuing to stare until I left the train three stops later, and new passengers boarding the train read the air and followed suit. For the second time in Japan I felt completely isolated and helpless, not fully understanding the events that just occurred on my seemingly boring morning commute to work.

Finally arriving at work, I enthralled my boss with the aforementioned events and he apologised wholeheartedly as if it were he that had committed this heinous act. He explained that by the description of the man's outfit, specifically the presence of the tattoo, it sounded like he was most likely a member of the Yakuza (Japanese Mafia).

He laughed when I told him I had practised this new and, perhaps in hindsight, inappropriately tame expression, and told me in a jovial manner that this was the incorrect use of such a phrase. Ki wo tsukete is only to be used when saying to somebody, 'Be careful', 'Take care', 'Look after yourself'. The nuance in the saying is usually to wish that someone stays safe in a possibly dangerous or troublesome situation (for example, whilst skiing down the side of a mountain…). In this instance I took the 'Be careful' translation literally. I meant to ask my attacker to watch out for my head but instead I essentially, rudely, told a dangerous man to 'watch himself'.

As you can imagine, my boss advised that the next time I see a man dressed likewise, I stand well away from him.

Sometimes it was very difficult to not stand out living there. I was accustomed to looks, stares and comments of all kinds, and had learned to embrace or act ignorant to it. I never expected such an unwarranted and unjustified attack of a cold Tuesday morning on the way to work.

Looking back, I can laugh at the fact that I thought I would defuse the situation by offering a simple helping of 'take care' post face-plant, and can happily report that this circumstance had not in any way tainted my love for this

117

country and its people.

There are 38 million people in the Greater Tokyo Area and I was just fortunate enough to meet the one bad guy who failed as an extra in a Clint Eastwood movie. It gave me an insight into how people reacted in certain situations, it gave me a chance to fail publicly at Japanese, and it gave me a stonker of an anecdote to regale colleagues with over our morning cup of coffee.

15

HANAMI

花見

Each year, at the end of March to the beginning of April, millions of people flood to Japan's parks, rivers, mountains, tree-lined streets or any place that lays home to the mighty sakura tree.

These people come laden with picnic baskets, alcoholic beverages, tarpaulin mats and whatever else they require, all with the same aim in mind: hanami. Hanami is the Japanese custom of flower viewing, in particular the cherry blossom or as it's known in Japan, sakura.

Cherry blossoms have become synonymous with Japan over the years, and it has become commonplace to find visitors climbing trees and lamp posts, crawling through shrubbery and long grass, or being tailed by hired professional photographers, all fighting to capture the perfect Instagram moment to share with the world.

Residents and tourists monitor the online and televised sakura forecast from the autumn and winter before, choosing the optimal time to travel to which specific park in which specific town or city, or even Japan itself if they're travelling from overseas.

The sakura trees usually stay in full bloom for a couple of weeks so timing is crucial. It's part of the mystique and fun of hanami as people will often camp out under the trees in order to reserve the best spot for their company or family outing in the most prolific areas. The Philosophers Path in Kyoto or Nakameguro in Tokyo are two popular spots that are full of visitors during this time.

Because of Japan's topography, the sakura blooms from the south to the north, so you will often find people travelling alongside them like migrating birds following the sun. I myself have enjoyed the sakura season a couple of times in the past but for my first year living in Japan, I enjoyed hanami in my favourite place with some very close friends.

After long deliberation, we had decided to partake in the flower fest in the famous Yoyogi Park, just next to Harajuku. Harajuku and Omotesando became our favourite places to shop and spend most of our free time, so Yoyogi seemed like the perfect place.

I had made a small group of expat friends from various Language Teaching events hosted throughout the city. As time passed, I would come to know their friends and in doing so formed a close-knit group with whom I would explore the city with every opportunity I had. Two such individuals, Dan and Rhianna, would become my closest friends, support network and overall rocks for my entire stay in Japan. Sharing common interests, including our love for Nintendo, studying Japanese, exploring new places, and our British heritage, the three of us became inseparable and would plan after work and weekend excursions whenever we could.

Yoyogi is one of the most eclectic places I've ever been. It's a biome of its own accord, where anybody can participate in any activity they wish (except for that... naughty). I would see artists painting, dancers dancing, dog walkers walking, actors acting, singers singing and archers... arching? Any animal that can be fitted with a harness will be walked, carried or pushed around in a pram. I've seen cats, dogs, rabbits, parrots, owls, ferrets, meerkats and squirrel monkeys to name a few casually on their daily outing.

The best thing about all this activity is that people can do as they like unscathed by judgement and comments from onlookers, for it is a free space where the arts and individuality are embraced.

The park is separated into many sections, be it lake, paths lined with trees, arboretum, dog park, boardwalk, fountain, the underside of a bridge where the dancers hang out, or open grasslands. We walked through the avenues of sakura trees glistening pink in the spring sun, treading carefully over the floor littered with soft pink confetti. Light beams pushing through the branches above created an ethereal pastel filter over picnickers, playing children and banquets below. Passing the hordes of happy (emotional and ethanol induced) campers, we selected an empty plot in an open field among fellow hanami-goers.

The plot we chose was essential, because as the park filled we began to realise we would be sitting there for life (meaning the end of the day) so the sun to shade ratio and distance from the public toilets were crucial. Satisfied with the acoustics and soil pH levels, we sprawled our belongings upon our ¥100 (70p) mats and soaked in the atmosphere.

Six hours of fun, rescuing Frisbees from trees, playing with strangers' pugs, chasing and popping man-sized bubbles, and downing gallons of umeshu (plum wine) later, the sun began to set and just Dan and I remained. We decided to make some new acquaintances so walked to the next island of people a mere ten feet from our camp.

Five minutes later, I returned to our camp to top up our beverages. Searching in the sudden pitch black through our belongings to locate my sweater, I shivered as the darkness brought on a cool breeze. My hands passed over Dan's SLR camera, Nintendo Switch console, some empty cartons of alcohol and packets of snacks to where my bag once sat. 'Once' being the operative word.

My bag was no longer MY bag.

Crap!

I remember as a kid begging my mother to drive extra fast

over the bridge on the way to my auntie's house because it would make the contents of my stomach jump at such a rate that it felt so unnatural yet had us gasping for more. The feeling in my stomach standing there in the dark park mimicked that feeling, except this time it was coupled with dread, confusion and a dash of panic.

Ok a lot of panic.

Only panic.

Calling Dan over, we surveyed the scene and decided that my bag and its contents were the only things missing. But how could this be so? We were in Japan, land of the safe, and only turned our backs for five minutes. People reserved their tables in restaurants with their phones, laptops, keys and deeds to their house. Theft was not a concept that existed.

I called the police in my drunken state, trying my utmost to explain what had happened, using the limited Japanese I could remember. Describing my location within the park was the most important factor, because within ten minutes or so, two police officers arrived and guided us to the nearest koban (police box), standing just outside the park's boundaries.

Trying and failing to act as sober as I could, I explained exactly what had transpired and described in great detail the contents of my bag. The officers were not really concerned with my possessions and didn't seem to grasp the severity of what had occurred. In fact, I was sure they didn't take me seriously in the slightest. Just another case of drunken tourists misplacing their belongings.

I leant over the table, removed the officer's pen from his shirt pocket and began drafting what can only be described as an elaborate collage of blueprints, carefully detailing the entire contents of my bag, equipped with labelled descriptions in both Japanese and English. Officers in the next room came a few steps closer to observe the chicken scratch and ramblings of a madman.

Living in Japan as an expat, it was imperative that I carried certain items with me at all times and it just so happened that each of these items were in my bag, most notably my Japanese resident's card.

Alongside this were my wallet containing my UK and Japanese bank cards, driver's licence and ID, my bank book, hanko (Japanese signature stamp), some clothes, USB stick with important files on, phone battery pack, keys to my apartment and some other bits. Not a good end to what had been a fantastic day in the park.

I explained that the monetary value of the contents was near to zero but the sentimental value was priceless. My wallet had belonged to and contained pictures of my grandfather and the bag itself was a leaving gift from my mother. Whomever stole my bag would have been hugely disappointed with their haul, and would have probably ditched all the insignificant items that meant so much to me but absolutely nothing to them.

Whilst sitting in the police station, two officers were sent to the park to perform an obligatory search of bushes, bins and toilets for signs of my missing bag. As the officers talked among themselves in another room, I contacted my bank in the UK to cancel my cards. When one of the officers returned, I presented him with my artwork and detailed descriptions. At the time, I felt I had hidden my intoxication quite well, but hindsight is both a curse and a blessing, and I feel that this time I may have misjudged the scene slightly.

The officer reluctantly took my work, and I turned back to Dan who had to leave, saying that he had an early start the next morning. As he left, he kindly handed me ¥5000 (£35) to last me the next couple of days, which I gratefully accepted. Another officer walked into the room to tell me that he had just heard back from the men in the park and that they had found nothing. They all agreed that the theft was the work of foreign tourists as this is the height of the tourist season, and was a very unlikely act for Japanese residents. Sadly, I agreed with them as I couldn't imagine this happening at any other time of the year in such a public setting.

Still somewhat inebriated and not trusting the word of the officers, I headed back through the park for one last search as I was convinced I would locate it or at least the emptied contents nearby. I found the spot where we had sat, noting the flattened grass and crumbs under the trees. This spot had been one of joy and fulfilment just hours before, and now it was an active crime scene. I felt like I should be collecting soil samples and blades of damaged grass to send back to the lab for further analysis.

Using the only possession on my person, I searched under the light of my phone like a madman digging for buried treasure under cover of darkness. The park was pitch black and as the last remaining bars of battery failed me I realised I was alone. Silence prevailed and the sound of the night hit me immediately; that sound of the soft wind that you only notice when the streets are empty and the moon is high in the sky. I found my way out of the park and walked back towards the station.

I made it only two stations on the train, and all the alcohol in my body decided that now was the time to evacuate. Returning from the bathroom, I noticed the platform was completely derelict. I had lost all track of time during my midnight hunt in the park, and had in fact now missed the last train home. Armed with a dead phone and a single ¥5000 note upon which to survive, I remembered a capsule hotel nearby that I had stayed in many years ago. Retracing steps from the past, I found the hotel with ease and for the first time that evening, I was in luck as there was a pod available for just under ¥5000.

Capsule hotels are an interesting concept. They were usually occupied by businessmen who desired nothing more than a cheap bed for the night. They have become something of a novelty, however, for foreigners due to those top 10 lists of crazy things to do in Japan, so you will often find groups of rowdy Europeans or American tourists returning from a night out on the lash.

Upon arrival, the concierge took my room ticket purchased at the entrance, and offered me a cult-esque set of brown robes to get changed into. Usually I would have had to leave all my belonging in a locker or behind the desk, but as I was unequipped, I walked straight on through to my 'room'.

Rows of spaceship-like aisles stood before me with double-tiered columns of pods within the walls. I was having flashbacks of all those crime shows I used to watch where they would pull out the cadaver on a cold slab from within the hospital's mortuary. I would be sleeping in a hole fit for a coffin.

Climbing into the capsule, I was reminded by how cosy they actually were. I had my own TV, plug sockets to charge my phone (if only I had a cable), and a bamboo blind to cover the entranceway. I passed out immediately from exhaustion.

Noises of shuffling and snoring clients woke me at around 5am, so I climbed down from my hole and slowly made my way back to the station to catch the first train home. After what seemed like the longest 24 hours of my life, I finally reached my apartment at around 6:30am and, luckily for me, just a couple of days before I'd had a momentary stroke of genius.

Looking at my spare key laying on the sideboard in the

kitchen, I questioned the purpose of owning such a thing. If I lost my key, I wouldn't be able to rectify the situation because the only useful spare key would be on the wrong side of the locked door. So, deciding on a healthy compromise, I sealed the key in an envelope and pushed it through my outside post box in the off chance that I should need it.

Present me thanked my past self for having such an innovative idea as I approached home dishevelled from the night's ordeal, twisted the combination lock and retrieved the shining beacon of hope from within.

I sat on my bed feeling violated and disappointed at myself for trusting strangers, and at the world for dealing me such a crappy card at the end of such a perfect day. I charged my phone and contacted my supervisor, telling him what had happened and that I would need to resolve the situation as soon as possible. He replied telling me not to worry about work, and that he would come meet me after lunch to help me out.

After an hour's nap to recharge my own batteries, I awoke and headed straight to my local police station to collect the Yoyogi police report and my case number required to reissue my resident's card. The policeman stared at me like I was a madman while I tried to explain in Japanese what I wanted. When at long last I succeeded, he disappeared and returned to tell me that the Yoyogi police hadn't filed the report and that I had to come back in a few days.

Later that afternoon, I met my supervisor who arrived with my case number in hand (he had been on the phone to both police stations for over an hour), and we then spent the rest of the day filling out forms and waiting in the city office to get my resident's card reissued.

He handed me an envelope containing ¥100,000 (£700) and told me to pay him back at my earliest convenience. I could have cried there and then at this selfless act of generosity. The past day had been one of intense and ever-changing emotions, and just when all appeared to be lost, he offered me the kindest token anyone could have offered.

The following day we left work early to visit the bank (they all closed at 5pm which was not so helpful when working a 9-5 job) to cancel and reissue my cards. I planned on also withdrawing the money I'd been lent to pay him back.

After a long and arduous meeting with the teller, I was informed that the bank could not allow me access to my own account or any of my own money until my new card had been issued. This new card would take two weeks to arrive! Two weeks with no money! If my supervisor hadn't been so kind as to lend me that money, I would have been royally screwed. What a completely ridiculous system.

Arriving home that evening, I received a letter from the Shinjuku police headquarters notifying me that my wallet had been found. It had been dumped in a bin in Shinjuku station (the largest station in the world) and somehow, somebody had noticed it and handed it in to the lost and found. Bless the Japanese people and their efficiency with lost items.

I travelled to the headquarters the following day and retrieved my wallet containing all my now cancelled cards, priceless pictures and all of ¥107 (£0.78) in change. I was blown away by the pure kindness and selflessness of the individual who had not only discovered my wallet sitting in a bin, but had taken the time to hand it into the authorities. This was only trumped by the most generous offer I have ever received in my entire life: the envelope of cash from my supervisor.

These two hugely meaningful acts restored my faith in the human race and flipped such a negative situation into one of growth and appreciation for the innate sense of kindness that really laid at the heart of this mega city.

The following year, I was a tad reluctant to attend hanami again only for history to repeat itself. My parents visited Japan from the UK and I am happy to say it was a much better experience the second time around.

The weather was perfect, the blossoms were perfect, the company was perfect, the food was perfect and the alcohol… well it was umeshu so what do you think? (The answer, is perfect.)

The park was full of families and friends enjoying the sunshine and revelling in the moment. Sitting under an avenue of trees bursting with blossoms, Dan and I, along with both of our families, chatted and laughed and told stories of our various travels, as pink petals rained down upon us. We ate and drank well into the evening, until the sun began to set. It was a flawless hanami experience all around, and a great introduction to this special custom for our families. A true Japanese tradition.

To end the day, Dan and I decided to take our parents for a walk along the famous sakura viewing spot on the Naka-Meguro river.

The river was lined with crowds ten people wide and we slowly wound our way across the many bridges along the river. I usually like to avoid crowds during seasons like this, but this was definitely a must-see and I was glad we could all experience it together.

Spotlights shone on the trees, illuminating the blossoms and covering the whole streets in a pink-red hue. Red lanterns hung among the branches, adding to the atmosphere as the hanami paparazzi adorned with cameras intensified the light display.

Even the local street cats were taking full advantage of all the commotion; perching atop the several statues and posts along the route, knowing full well that visitors would pay them attention and perhaps offer them some food. Naturally the lines to see the cats overtook those for the blossoms, and my parents were able to see yet another Japanese marvel unfold before their eyes. Cat-viewing.

This was how hanami should be and should have been the previous year. I am glad that my tainted version is now but an anecdote that I can look upon with a shouganai attitude, and that the second year's revived version can be looked upon with nothing but fondness. For it truly was the perfect day, spent with the perfect company in the perfect location.

16

TADAIMA PART FIVE

ただいま#5

Changes

Living in a Japanese apartment can pose many questions and problems to the occupant, and these will quite often vary throughout the year. My apartment could be a sensitive soul and with each seasonal change came new aspects of my home that I had never realised or acknowledged before.

Summers created saunas, winters created igloos and weekend lay-ins became a distant memory of the past. I have gleaned a lot from my stay in my apartment and it certainly taught me a lot about my strengths, weaknesses and levels of resilience. Having experienced each season three times through both living in and visiting Japan, I shall depict what I view to be an accurate account of each, and how it affected my living conditions.

Summer

夏

During my first Japan visit in the summer of 2005 I, along with seven other students, travelled the length and breadth of the country for three weeks throughout June and July, starting in Hokkaido and ending in Kyushu, stopping along the way in Fukushima, Yokohama and Hiroshima respectively.

We stayed with different families in each location and adopted the lifestyle of a Japanese high school student. Each house and school varied in many ways from the next and the further south we travelled, the more the heat and humidity levels intensified. Hokkaido was hot but Kyushu was on another level. I remember it being almost 40°C in the shade at one point and hanging my head out of a car window achieved nothing; no breeze, no refreshing coolness; just tangibly thick, hot air.

I distinctly remember sleeping in a room with no glass windows; just a big hole in the wall in a small house in Oita. There were bugs in the bed and so I opted to sleep on the floor under the bed. Sleeping on the floor is commonplace for many people in Japan, especially in traditional houses with tatami mats. Futons replace beds and they are easily folded away to open up the room during the day. I would often hear women taking all their anger of the year out on their futons on a nice sunny day. If I peered up on my daily walk, I would see them draping the beds over balconies smacking all the dust, bugs and hair out with large paddles, allowing it to rain down like detritus.

Living on the outskirts of Tokyo during the summer months was very different to the summer I had spent all those years ago in Kyushu, but renting my own place was a whole new ball game. With the heat, came more heat that was absorbed and captured by the buildings, making it unbearable.

Temperatures in Tokyo tend to reach highs of 29°C (that's not to say there aren't some weeks when it is 36°C every day) and lows of 22°C. Returning home at the end of the day it was not uncommon to find that it was 5°C hotter inside than it was outside. My air conditioning unit became my best friend during these months, and I even purchased a portable fan with a remote control that I would leave on throughout the night. I found that after a while I needed the white noise in the background in order to fall asleep soundly. It became a new comfort of mine.

Summers in Japan are usually accompanied by nice cool showers. I would close each door inside my apartment and spend all of my time locked in my bedroom where the air conditioning unit was located. I ate, slept, dressed and got ready in said room until I was ready to brace the intense heat outside. Leaving the apartment and walking down the four flights of stairs was enough exposure to cover my entire body in a layer of sweat.

Coming from the UK, I am not a person who particularly perspires profusely (try saying that five times in a row), but during the summer months, I accepted the inevitable and refused to go anywhere without what I had dubbed my 'Sweat Rag'. Hand towels are attached to each person throughout the heat, used to wipe brows, shade heads from the sun and to clean hands after washing them. These, along with 'sunbrellas' and the free plastic fans given out by each shop were imperative survival tools I wouldn't go anywhere without in the bleak and harsh heat.

Heat brought on waves of flying and crawling critters. I found the sound of cicadas synonymous with Japan and welcomed their arrival with open arms. Insects have always fascinated me and occasionally one would land on my balcony where I revelled in being able to observe it up close. The light directly above my front door attracted all types of night crawlers and quite often I found myself being woken by the sound of continual thudding against my door as they fell from the sharp jabs of the bulb. In the morning, I walked out onto an insect graveyard, stepping carefully over stunned and dying luminous green beetles and moths of all shapes and sizes. I had to fight my inner saviour's urge to pick them all up and nurse them back to health.

Mosquitos were an ever-present nuisance this time of year. I am an avid lover of all life but if I were to choose to eradicate one species from the earth it would be the mosquito. I happen to be one of those unfortunate individuals deemed as a deliciously succulent meal to the little blood thieves. Simply walking to the local combini would leave me covered in small wounds. My joints appeared to be the most appetising as I was constantly finding bumps all around my ankles, wrists, elbows and knees.

During the night, I sometimes heard the lucky one that managed to break into my apartment as it circled my head, and thus began the nightly hunt for the culprit, only ceasing as its life does. I once ventured into Ueno Zoo with my friends in the height of the summer, and this setting along with the added heat from the animals was enough to attract a disgustingly unpleasant number of mosquitos. We were actively swatting them off our entire body for the entire morning. My friend's phone was covered in little spots of blood where she'd used it as a weapon. We ended up being chased out of the zoo prematurely.

Autumn

秋

The end of summer brings about the end of the deathly heat wave and I was no longer fearful of leaving my apartment. I could once again wear grey clothes without fear of sweat patches and I bid farewell to shorts and welcomed the strange clinging sensation of jeans once more.

The leaves began to change and people now flocked in their millions to the nearest mountain, hill, forest or tree to marvel in their splendour. Japan knows how to put on a seasonal show and it seems all the trees were planted hundreds of years ago with futuristic leaf viewing in mind. Shades of browns, reds, oranges and yellows blend into each other with perfect transition as everything suddenly feels right with the world. It's not yet cold enough to snuggle into my winter attire but I found myself adding on more layers and enjoying the comfort of regulating my own body temperature. The air is cooler and fresher and I could begin to enjoy nature once more, becoming a professional hiker in a morning and exploring unknown territories.

Insects and small critters are still prevalent and are now seeking inner warmth from houses and accommodation alike, so it was imperative to utilise the screened doors and windows. Condensation became my worst adversary as I began to switch on my heater for the first time in a while, especially during the many typhoons that hit the islands.

Typhoons to some strike images of falling trees, floods and destruction aplenty. To me, it brought back memories of the UK, and quite often meant a day off work to lounge around the house wallowing in my own filth; stuffing my face and catching up on Netflix. During our first year we had a week-long super typhoon, and Dan and I constructed a nest in my living room and did nothing but play games for hours on end, listening to the howling winds prevailing outside.

138

What a treat.

Even as a child I adored thunderstorms and the sound of rain. I like knowing that I am safe under my duvet or warm inside my house as Mother Nature takes her toll outside. In Japan however, when the wind blew, my entire apartment shook. It was extremely sensitive so I felt everything – from wind to lorries passing by … to earthquakes.

During my first few months in Japan, I took note of the time and place I was whenever I experienced an earthquake. I added this to the back of my Journal of Firsts and over the course of my stay there it became habitual to take a screenshot of my phone each time I felt an earthquake, later adding it to the ever-growing list. On average, I felt one earthquake every two weeks.

Most of the earthquakes were small; my friends hardly ever noticed them like I did. I only experienced two notably large earthquakes during my time there; one of which issued a tsunami warning.

It was the morning of November 22nd 2016. I was awoken abruptly at 6am by my doors shaking and vibrating loudly. My bed began to thrust about, not just up and down as was often the case, but side to side. I instantly jolted upright and opened all of the doors.

We were told in training to open all doors in case the building collapses and you are trapped inside. In doing so I could see my utensils swaying in the kitchen and many pots and pans fell onto the floor which startled me even more. I didn't know what to do or where to go if it continued. The whole thing lasted about fifteen-twenty seconds which was a very long time for my brain to go into overload. Usually they only lasted three-five seconds, hardly noticeable at all, but this one was different. I could feel it approaching like a train; noting the ripples as it spread underground.

As my apartment rumbled around me, not knowing what to do, I instantly jumped to a group messaging service I had with my friends back home, as I knew they would be able to calm me down. At the same time, my phone lit up with warnings from the government and also from a private messaging service I had with my company. They sent through details of a tsunami warning issued by the Japanese government and announced that the earthquake had struck Fukushima and measured 7.4 at first and was later lowered to 6.9 on the Richter scale. This was far higher than the drastic earthquake that hit in 2011. That occurrence was initially measured at 7.1 but was later lowered to 6.6. Realising this, I began to panic even further as fear of the unknown took over.

This earthquake was said to be an aftershock of the 2011 earthquake and in fact did cause a tsunami of 1.5 meters. This was of course nowhere as big as the waves of 2011, but fifteen people were still injured, three of which were seriously hurt. In comparison it was a tiny blip, especially when you compare it to the almost 16,000 people who lost their lives in 2011 and the further 8000 people who were either injured or missing.

However, on a personal note from someone who is from a country where our biggest natural concerns are adders and the rain, it was terrifying to receive warnings of potential chaos and devastation via text message.

Thousands of thoughts whizzed through my mind a mile a second and that feeling of hopelessness is something I wish to never experience again. Contacting my friends in the UK only made them worry and demand that I jump on the first plane home which just made me feel guilty for worrying them.

I would come to learn that the warnings I received were only precautionary and have since researched to discover exactly what it was I was supposed to do in case of a real emergency. I should have had a supply kit ready to leave at all times, and headed towards my local school. I will admit I didn't have the kit but I at least knew where to go which was the first step.

Aside from the threat of natural disasters, living in Japan in the autumn was relatively comfortable and easy going. I could once again use my entire apartment and I didn't have to worry about temperature control. Temperatures in Tokyo reach average highs of 22°C and lows of 15°C and it was by far one of the easiest times of the year to live in my apartment.

Winter

冬

Winter. What can I say about winter? I love winter. I love snow. I love snow days. I love wrapping up warm and wearing scarves and gloves. I love my thick, comfortable winter jacket and my snug winter boots. I did not, however, love living in Japan during winter!

Winter in a Japanese apartment meant no sleep, constant shivering and illnesses. It meant freezing when outside and sweating and stripping off in the blasting heat of the crowded trains, which only added to the pending illnesses. It once again meant locking myself in my bedroom with the air conditioning unit, in order to feel the benefits of its heating function.

Sleeping was difficult and it was commonplace for me to sleep wearing thick tracksuit bottoms and a thick jumper whilst under my duvet, topped with a kotatsu blanket. Kotatsu are Japanese tables that house a small heater on the underside. The top is usually heavy and removeable, enabling the owner to place a huge thick blanket underneath. Owners and guests alike gather around and sit under the blanket, basking in the trapped heat from beneath. People often sleep under their kotatsu in the winter months. I couldn't afford one at the time so opted for the blanket instead and used it as a duvet topper.

Waking up in the mornings was always a struggle, especially when I could see my own breath whilst walking into the kitchen. On occasion, I would open the fridge and be shocked to feel warmth coming from it. My phone notified me that during these times temperatures read -5°C inside my apartment. On average, winter temperatures in Tokyo reach highs of 10°C and lows of 2°C in the daytime and much less in the evenings. In conclusion, winter mornings are not fun.

In the summer, I enjoyed eating light, cold meals, so rarely utilised my electrical appliances, but during the first winter in my new apartment, I became dependent on them, only to have a meltdown when one of them failed on me. My tiny camping stove and fish grill didn't pack much heat but was sufficient enough to cook up a mean spaghetti bolognese. That was until the life slowly drained from it midway through frying some meat.

At first, I thought there was a problem with the gas tap at the back, so I unplugged and reconnected it (the old off-and-on-again procedure). Next, I thought maybe too much gas was leaking so left it ten minutes and tried again. I concluded that I had been dealt a dodgy article and laid the blame solely on the realtor who sold it to me. Bit harsh.

I threw the meat away and spent the next few weeks living off bento boxes from the supermarket, as I was too busy with work to arrange someone to come collect and replace my now broken stove.

Eventually I contacted the real estate company with a well-written letter of complaint, describing my angst after being provided with a broken appliance. The response was a very blunt, "It's not us, it must be something you're doing wrong!"

I didn't care for this answer so asked them to replace it as soon as possible as I was unable to feed myself sufficiently. They replied that the batteries must need changing.

"It's a stove! There are no batteries," I replied.

This slow back and forth conversation transpired over a week or so until eventually they sent me a picture of my stove's manual of instructions where it clearly depicted a secret compartment that opened in the front, allowing access to the battery slot.

Oops.

After returning home from the combini with a pack of huge batteries, I inserted them into the secret slot, turned on the ignition and the fire was real! Flames erupted from it like a volcano.

Another beautiful piece of equipment I had always appreciated was my thinking throne. Growing up, if I or a family member ever lost anything or couldn't remember something, my grandmother would ask Saint Anthony, Patron Saint of Lost Items. The only way this would work, she said, was if you sat on the thinking throne. So off she

144

would trot to perch upon her ceramic muse, until the answer came to her which miraculously had a ninety-nine per cent success rate.

Toilets in Japan have more powers than just that of recall. If you were lucky, they would come equipped with buttons aplenty. Mine had a lovely row of opportunities to choose from. There was the standard jet shower to clean the back, the bidet function to clean the front, I could even control the power and temperature of the jet as well as the duration of the stream. Then there was my favourite function, the heated seat. Yes, no longer did I fear cold toilet seats during the harsh winter months and this simple feat of engineering would bring me joy upon waking up on those frosty mornings. The seat was constantly warm for my liking and upon sitting, would sense my presence and warm up even more. Throughout the winters I would bring books aplenty and music to listen to just for the pure enjoyment. It's the little things in life.

This seat of wonders wasn't always my friend though, for on the day after I moved into my apartment we got into a bit of an altercation. I was issued a check list of things to run through upon moving in, checking the functionality and quality of all features in the apartment. One item included the buttons on the toilet. Simple, one might think.

Sitting down I heard the seat react to my weight. Looking down at the row of buttons, I pressed the one nearest me and heard the mechanisms churning. Seconds later I felt a directed stream of cold water in the correct area. I proceeded to test out the water temperature and the bidet functions (all for the checklist of course). Surprisingly, this actually felt good. It was definitely an unnatural feeling, but I could see the practicality and decided this was a sensation I could definitely get used to. I had deemed my new friend and all his buttons worthy, pressing the big stop button for the finale, with thoughts now directed towards the next item on the list.

Except nothing happened. I must have missed. I pressed it once more. The jet continued to spray.

'Ok, maybe I didn't press it hard enough,' I thought, 'try it one more time.'

I started to panic.

'What if I can't turn it off? It'll go all over the walls and floor. The wallpaper is wafer thin and it'll peel off. I can't call somebody for help, especially the landlord. He already thinks I'm a crazy foreigner who doesn't know what trash is. What would he say if he discovered I'm not fully toilet trained as well? Unacceptable. Ok think, think, think.

'THINK!

'What do I usually do when technology stops working? Blow on it? It's not a Sega Mega Drive. That won't help here. Turn it off and on again? Tried that, didn't work. Unplug it and plug it back in again? Toilets don't have plugs!

'Oh, wait!' I noticed a plug. 'My toilet has a plug?!'

I reached down and carefully unplugged it. The water ceased and the jet receded back into the basin. Hallelujah. Saved by technology logic from the 1990's!

Spring

The passing of winter and the arrival of spring once again assembles masses of tourists as barren landscapes transform into avenues of candy floss covered trees, welcoming the overnight transition into sakura season.

Snow days are sporadic and temperatures fluctuate at a menopausal rate from bone achingly freezing to almost t-shirt friendly in a single twenty-four hours. Spring temperatures around Tokyo reach average highs of 18°C and lows of 7°C although the evenings can be unkind, reaching below 0°C with a feel factor of much less with the strong winds.

As February slides into March, I would finally allow myself to pull down the towel pinned to my kitchen window, acting as a draft excluder, allowing beams of light to once again penetrate my apartment. The screen doors to my balcony could be dusted down and the cool fresh air emanated throughout my apartment, dancing around the rooms, eradicating any signs of mustiness. The sun made its sparkling return from hibernation and being outside was no longer a chore, for Vitamin D was once again free on the menu.

I could fold up my kotatsu blanket and lay it across the sofa which could also now be used again as the sun permitted access to the entire apartment. I would no longer have to sprint from my bedroom to the bathroom and back in the mornings. I could enjoy a leisurely stroll across my kitchen and sing wholeheartedly under the warm water of my shower without fear of shrinking back into myself the second it was turned off.

Friends came over for dinner and games parties more often and everybody seemed happier in spirit. I used to love how the sunshine and lighter days could do that to people. I used to work nights and the sun was a rare sight for me then. I would wake up as it set and go to sleep as it rose. Staff members would often be sick or suffer from seasonal affective disorder. There was little access to windows and the ones you did pass were blacked out by the night sky; this in turn lowered team morale and group mentality noticeably.

Spring in Japan was a happy time of year for me. Everything was sakura flavoured, everybody carried a camera as once boring trees converted into celebrity status and I just felt lighter as I no longer had to worry about wearing thick winter coats, scarves and hats.

Living in Tokyo throughout the spring was my favourite because the days became warmer and longer, and I constantly had something to look forward to. Sleeping was easier and I truly appreciated and embraced living in a larger place. I like open spaces and I could really manipulate the light and air flow around my apartment. In all, it was the happiest time of the year and brings forth the happiest of memories when I look back on my time in my apartment.

Weekends

週末

Weekends in Tokyo could be an interesting experience in itself. For the traveller or tourist, weekends are usually the time when they hit up Harajuku to see all the otaku fans dressed up, it's when events are held and one can enjoy recording the crowds at the famous Shibuya crossing.

For the resident, however, weekends outside were something to be avoided. Harajuku and Shinjuku were two places I visited on a bimonthly basis but at the weekends, they were impossible to navigate. I found myself becoming extremely frustrated with the flocks of people idly prancing about, taking pictures and posing by every sign, shop and tree.

Walking through the high street to my favourite art shop could take me almost an hour on a weekend when it would usually take five minutes on a weekday. It was not that I disliked people (part of me did), but after a while I lost that sense of awe for the new and just wanted to arrive somewhere, run an errand and move onto the next place at ease.

Sleeping in on a weekend could also prove a difficult task. I was lucky in that where I lived, I did not suffer from sound pollution from traffic or people, but I did suffer from something much worse. Sirens.

Sound trucks coasted through the streets each Saturday and Sunday between 8am-12pm. Trucks adorned with loudspeakers advertised second hand DVDs and TV collections, electoral candidates and their policies, sweet potatoes and anything else, to their heart's desire. Even ambulances and fire trucks sounded their alarms whether sitting in traffic or not. They would drive around the tight back streets at a very slow pace with sirens blasting no matter the time. Even when stopping or stationary outside a house, the sirens were kept on. This was not fun for those of us that resided next door to an elderly home where ambulances were commonplace.

Doing a food shop on a weekend was a brave task for those who did not love waiting in line for half an hour, arriving at the counter with a basket of thawed out frozen vegetables. I would return home with heavy bags dripping with condensation and was greeted by door salesmen from the television licence company NHK. They were not the friendliest of folk and even after attempting to notify them that I did not own a TV, or in my case pretended to not understand any Japanese, I had no choice but to just close the door on them and wait patiently for them to leave the premises. I soon became aware of which parts of my floor creaked, allowing me to tip-toe across my apartment to peek through the hole in my door before electing to open it or to creep back in, hoping they hadn't heard any signs of life from inside.

I liked to visit parks and unpopulated places at the weekends, especially if the sun was out. I liked to keep a list of places I had still yet to visit so weekends would be a nice time to tick them off, or try foods I had never eaten before. Either that or weekends for many became days for household chores and errands like any other grown-up with a nine-to-five job.

So, there you have it. As each season passed, new changes occurred both in my apartment and in myself, and I found myself adjusting in an almost symbiotic way. I suppose it did add character to my accommodation.

17

TRAIN CHRONICLES #6

電車物語#6

TGIF

The week is over and the weekend ahead of me; the evening is mine and the city is waiting for me. Fridays were everyone's favourite days. I could just feel the air thin and morale lift throughout the office as everyone was silently rejoicing at the upcoming two-day break.

Leagues of people flooded into the city's bars, restaurants, arcades and shopping malls, releasing that pent-up anxiety and energy from the long, tiresome and busy week they'd had.

Friday night turned into an out-out night of drinking, dancing, arcades, throwing up in back alleys or having a power nap on any tangible surface. Then at last leagues of people, now spread throughout the entire city of Tokyo, would unite in a single moment : they would all be taking the last train home.

The last train, depending on where I was and which line I would be taking could be anywhere from 12-1am and if I missed it, the first train wasn't until 5am in most places which meant the dedication of pulling an all-nighter, booking a hotel or what a lot of people tended to do, sleep in McDonalds until daybreak.

I personally resided on the outskirts of the city so usually had to think about ending my night around 11:40pm if I wished to catch the connecting trains that took me all the way home. This was always a tough decision each time I went out or visited friends over the weekend period.

The closer the evening got to the final train, the more manic the stations became, and the more fun or terrifying the trains could be depending on how I viewed things (or how intoxicated I was). Passengers adopted the squeeze and push approach entering the carriages; reversing into the train, securely gripping the top of the door frame with one hand until the doors began to close, then pushing back with all the force they could muster until safely contained within the vehicle. This process then continued to worsen with each passing station.

During the week, trains were places of silence and peace, but over the weekend, with the help of some trusty ethanol-based products, these metal tubes on tracks came alive. Riders forgot the access and availability of handrails or rings, and suddenly hundreds of individuals were morphed into one solid mass, swaying and falling as one, as the train twisted and turned along the tracks. I was shocked if I did not see or smell vomit, or witness at least forty bright red faces of salary men gripping cans of Strong Zero.

On one occasion, I was gifted with tiny splatters of second-hand Friday night dinner and drinks all over my brand-new shoes as I stood patiently on the train one evening. A young gentleman was smoothly ejecting his evenings consumptions into a plastic bag complemented with holes and tears. His friends, passed out next to him, swayed to and fro in unison with the train. My reflexes got the best of me as I swerved just in time to receive the appetiser before avoiding the main course, dessert and cheese board. Other passengers were not as amused as I was, and as the scent drifted throughout the carriage, the crowd dispersed like ants.

The train finally reached my station and I headed straight in the direction of the male toilets to clean up my shoes. Entering the bathroom, I cleared my dry throat and subsequently startled yet another ever so slightly merry gentleman going about his bathroom duties.

For fear of over detailing the event, the man was positioned at the urinal in a most unorthodox manner, with his arms behind his back held out to the sides slightly, and his groin thrust forward at an angle, quite sufficient for his current post.

In the process of being startled by my entrance, he turned to look at the source of the noise, but rather than turning his head as a sober man of the world, he chose to rotate his entire body, expelling his broken seal all over the floor and my vomit splattered shoe. What did my shoe ever do to deserve such negative attention of a Friday evening?

The gravity of his actions failed to register in his mind, and he modestly reversed back into position, all the while continuing to reject his lengthy stream of recycled Strong Zero.

Friday nights. The one night of the week where innocent personality and manner purges could take place, and where residing expats were offered a glimpse into the true mindset of locals and how their habits were affected by low inhibitions. The controlled chaos of the last train home will always stand at the forefront of the very best memories of my time in Japan.

18
KANPEKI

完璧

One thing I had always wanted to try, but never quite knew how to, was acting. I find the whole industry extremely fascinating and had always wondered what it would be like to appear in some form of media, be it on the small screen or big. Unbeknownst to me, this pipedream of mine would finally present itself in the form of a Japanese commercial.

During April 2017, the Japanese branch of a highly reputable and world-famous audit firm began casting their upcoming recruitment and advertising commercial. Each role had been cast, except, that was, for 'foreign accountant'. Employees were told to reach out among their non-Japanese resident friends, and the recommendation made its way through one of my colleagues and onto me. I gratefully accepted the proposal and contacted the company immediately.

I sent them descriptions of my height and weight along with a few pictures of myself in a suit. They responded very quickly with a time and date to meet with their English-speaking representative who would guide me through the day.

A few days later, I arrived at Yurakucho station early to meet the representative, with whom I travelled to the final destination in Tsukishima. I had no idea where we were going or exactly what I would be doing. I put all my trust in this woman and just told myself I wasn't in the UK anymore and that I could trust people more here. Not everyone was out to scam me. This was a respected company.

This self-given pep talk was especially helpful as we arrived on the manmade island, surrounded by working docks full of old cargo boats and winding streets laden with huge warehouses. I kept asking her where we were going and at each corner she would state that we were nearly there. Rounding yet another corner, we walked through a narrow alley to stop at a loading bay, which I was instructed to climb, and step into the foyer of an office block.

I was led through an empty lobby and reception area, into a vast open space behind a large glass door. Straightaway I was welcomed by a small team of people all awaiting my arrival. I took in the room: a huge green clothed stage lay at the back of the space with green walls, floor and ceiling. A lone table and three chairs stood at the left side of the stage. A small room off to the left was buzzing with excitement and my curiosities began to stir. I craned my neck around the door to see what was happening inside, and was startled as somebody called out my name from behind.

I followed the voice and was introduced to a panel of young professionals who I assumed were all of some importance. It turned out that I was standing before the director and his crew. I noticed right away how relaxed and informal their demeanour and appearances were, which relaxed me instantly. Dressed in black baggy tracksuit bottoms and casual plain t-shirts, wearing edgy and inventive hairstyles reminiscent of Parisian art students, they all certainly looked the part.

I was advised to take a seat next to the two smartest dressed men in the building and was introduced to my co-workers for the day. Both actors were also wearing business suits. The accountant trio was complete. I bowed and gave a brief introduction in Japanese. They asked me what acting experience I had, and I unabashedly told them this was my first job. They seemed impressed at my bravery, but as they went on to list the commercials, soap operas and movies on their resumes, I realised I may have misread benevolence for commiseration.

The two suited men were called into the small room to the left, leaving me sitting by myself, not knowing what to do or what would happen next. A woman and a man left the room and replaced the two that had just left. I recognised the new man from many of the adverts played on the trains. The woman told me she was an actress too and had made appearances in soap operas and small movies. My happy-go-lucky attitude soon turned into one of fear and nerves. I was among professionals and was a complete amateur.

What had I gotten myself into?

Finally, my name was called and I was directed into a chair between the other two men who were both having makeup applied to their faces.

'So, this is what all the commotion was about. I am now in hair and makeup,' I thought. 'Wait, makeup? Is this really necessary? I don't want to be one of those shiny people you see all over the adverts on the trains. I can never decipher if they are real or computer generated.'

Evidently, it was extremely necessary for us all to wear makeup as it prevented the studio lights from reflecting from our faces. The resident makeup artist applied concealer to my face and I have to admit that it actually made my skin look so much clearer and fresher. I was a new man. Finally, I understood why women all over the world lathered on this stuff in the gallons. This would be a one-off and I allowed myself to enjoy it while its effects lasted.

The stylist moved onto my hair and as soon as her fingertips made contact, she let out a little piglet-like squeal and ran out of the room into the main hall.

'What did I do? Did I have lice? Was I the latest unwitting host of Lord Voldemort?'

The other two men were giggling to themselves at a joke that everyone was in on except me, until a gaggle of women appeared in the room and all began caressing my hair,

stroking and tugging at it whilst uttering rounds of loud
"EEEEEEEEEEEEEEHHH?!"

'OK this madness has to end! What the hell is going on?' I
thought to myself.

The English-speaking representative finally joined the
groom-fest and informed me that none of the stylists had
ever touched a foreigner's hair before and that mine is the
softest they have ever felt. This had been the cause of all the
commotion and she then ran her hands through my hair to
confirm that it was indeed soft. I guess soft hair is now
something I can add to my resume.

I was issued a storyboard of the entire commercial and tried
to decipher what the plan actually was, seeing as I still knew
absolutely nothing about my role or the theme of the
commercial. By the looks of it, every other person in the
room knew exactly what their role and duties were. I was
informed that the storyboard had notes and instructions to
each cast member from the director, so spent the next
twenty minutes frantically trying to read his chicken-scratch
handwriting and frantically typing it all into a translation
app.

Awkward introductions. Check.

Hair and make-up. Check.

Brief briefing. Check.

So far so good.

Myself and the two other accountants were whisked over to the green stage where the table and chairs stood, and were directed to our allotted seats. As the director took the lead actors to the right to go over their markers, the representative came by to finally fill me in on the story and in particular, my role.

It turned out that I was playing one of three accountants working for a futuristic version of the company. A new client (the man from the train adverts) was being shown around the company by the manager (the woman) who would show him data on the company's futuristic technology. She would walk over to the table where we were each to show her our findings, which she would then relay back to the client, leaving him satisfied with our service.

I was notified that whilst the camera was facing the table, it will be focused on the three of us with myself in the centre. We were to be engaged in conversation when the boss arrived and cease when she is seated. Holographic graphs and charts were to be hovered above the table, and in turn we were expected to each enthusiastically present our findings. As she then walks away, we should be seen rejoicing in her acceptance. There was to be a voiceover with music over the entire rolling clip which would need to be shot in one take. We were advised to speak out loud when on camera to make us appear to be actually speaking rather than miming.

'Ok', I thought to myself, 'just sit at the table and murmur any nonsensical Japanese words to the two other men. The woman will sit down to hear what we have to say. I will await my turn to point to an imaginary chart above the table, which for whatever reason, I am delighted about. She will acknowledge our pretend figures and walk away, at which point I will turn to my comrades and celebrate. I will then ramble more incomprehensible waffle as the camera pans away. Got it. That can't be too difficult, can it?'

We began rehearsals at once and practised a couple of run-throughs to thoroughly understand the timing. The voiceover played over a loudspeaker so we knew when to move onto each section. I took cues from the other guys and followed suit, as I had no idea what I was doing the whole time. They took it very seriously and it inspired me to do the same. I wasn't laughing inside as I usually would in these types of moments and continuously wondered how I could document the moment unseen.

The camera man appeared on stage, rigged up to some kind of transformers robot with a camera on the end. It was controlled by his body and the word gyroscope kept whizzing through my mind as he supported the mechanisms unburdened by gravity. I remember thinking what a funny word gyroscope was and played a mental game of 'how many words can I make from the word gyroscope?' This surprisingly calmed my nerves and made me appear more focused, even if my mind was now deducing whether or not 'Spyro' was an acceptable contender for my game.

After ten or so practice runs, we stopped for a lunch of bento boxes and green tea. The other actors all went for a cigarette break and I was consulted by the representative who told me I was doing a good job and to keep up what I was doing (I was sure they had no idea what to do with me but I looked at the glass as half full and decided that yes, in fact, I was doing a marvellous job).

I had a brief chat with the other guys at my table and took a cheeky picture of the three of us. One of them told me I must never show this picture to anyone else, because he was famous and didn't want his fans to see any behind-the-scenes pictures on the internet. On the train ride home, I really wished I'd written down their names so I could cyber stalk them, but there truly was no time in all the commotion.

Lunch ended and we were herded back into position, where we perfected the scene for five more hours until the director finally shouted, "CUT!" He approached me and shouted in my face, "KANPEKI!" I'd heard this word before but couldn't quite recall the meaning until I double checked later on and discovered it meant 'perfect'. I wish I knew at the time as I wouldn't have acted so shocked and innately offended at actually doing a good job.

The actors and crew all gathered around the computer screen to watch the final take before uniting in a circle for a final briefing and a sincere "Good job" from the director. We collected our things and bid each other a hearty farewell. I left with my makeup still intact, not entirely sure what had just transpired. Had I truly performed exceptionally? Would they secretly replace me and reshoot the entire piece another day? Could this be my break into Hollywood? I doubted it. Tim Burton wouldn't be calling me anytime soon based on that performance.

Four months later, I finally received the completed commercial and was blown away by the CGI effects and final edit. They managed to turn it into a three-minute-long story of the evolution of auditing along with our segment at the end. The hologram bursting out the of the table along with all the other CGI effects looked incredible and reminded me of something from a science-fiction movie. Clearly the budget for this commercial was much higher than I realised.

I am very proud to be a part of this project and to have a copy of the commercial to keep as a memento of my time in Japan. It was a real experience that not many of my peers had achieved, and is one that I'll cherish always. I am pleased that I had the opportunity to taste the life of an actor for a day, and can happily retire before my head gets any bigger than it needs to be. That, and I couldn't handle the groupies.

19

BETSU BETSU

別々

Standing in the street with Dan and Rhianna and some other friends one afternoon in April, we began to notice people lining up behind us. As more people joined the growing mass, we realised they had mistaken our 'queue' as a sign that something was worth seeing.

Was this really happening? 'Do people really believe we are in line for some amazing event?' I thought. Whatever happened to free-thinking and individualism?

出る釘は打たれる 'The nail that stands out must be hammered down.' This blunt expression is one that lies at the basis of Japanese life and culture. It is carefully and suggestively woven into society to the point where when questioned about its presence, most are oblivious or confounded by the notion.

I have queried the proverb with Japanese colleagues and

friends, and most usually acknowledged the expression in an unassuming or humbled nature; neither denying nor commenting on the phrase with negative connotation.

Way of life in Japan was paired with enforced and unquestioned rules and regulations that detailed each aspect of one's daily routines. Both religion and culture played a part in this carefully set, unspoken lifestyle conditions.

Individuality as a concept is a strange and bewildering attribute that is subliminally suppressed by the masses as most people go about their day. I was witness to several incidences where the individual was publicly denoted as a rebel and quickly forced to repress all spontaneity for fear of further shame.

I worked with colleagues who were denied use of their unique and slightly westernised characteristics and whom were ostracised to the back of the staffroom and shunned so much for doing so that they were encouraged to seek employment elsewhere. All this despite the incredible work ethic and incomparable results gained from their departments.

I witnessed schoolgirls being scolded for daring to dye their hair a single tone of dark brown lighter than their natural colour, and dare I mention the treatment of tattoos in any public domain, notably public baths? Access was denied to all who had tainted their bodies with such an impure act. Luckily, as an expat, this rule rarely applied to me on the grounds of cultural differences.

In essence, I observed people in Japan being taught from infancy that the needs of the group hugely outweighed that of the individual. It was therefore intrinsically practised from adolescence into adulthood to the point where this trait had become common behaviour within social construct.

My initial reaction to the plethora of rules in Japan was always that of humour and curiosity, but after living there for over two years, I ended up finding my patience and common sense tested daily. Simple yes/no questions extended into lengthy debates, basic requests to an individual entered hierarchical realms, and complete nonsensical actions were justified with: "but it's the rules".

Along with other expats living in Japan, I coined my own expression to cover such peculiarities:

'Because Japan': an *expression* used to describe the unexplainable occurrences within Japan.

"Why do you have to give your landlord a mandatory gift of one month's rent on top of the one month's rent deposit before you move into your apartment?" my mother asked me once.

"Well... because Japan," I answered in a matter-of-fact manner.

This expression had become commonplace among my group of friends when encountering and attempting to

167

explain something out of the ordinary.

There were several situations and examples I observed every day, some of which frustrated me but most of which entertained me.

The first instance of following-and-acting-with-the-masses has to be the excessive amount of queuing that took place. At first, I thought that it was just part and parcel of living in Tokyo, but after travelling all over Japan, I had come to realise that it was in fact a custom in itself. As briefly touched on before, I would find people queuing for literally anything: a new food item that signs stated was the best thing since sliced bread, an event of any kind, any type of exclusive item, shop or arcade machine, a premiere to a movie, show or play, anything remotely famous or idol group related (don't even get me started on idol groups!), escalators or just another queue that looked like it could lead somewhere exciting.

Theme parks were also interesting places where I would encounter lengthy queues. Playing the single-rider game was always fun because no-one wanted to stand out and skip the entire queue only to ride alone, so I quite often found myself in luck there.

Escalators were where people were at their worst. Going about life at a steady and easy pace seemed to be the way of life there, so walking up an escalator was seen as 'rushing'. This had led way to the insanity and chaos that transpired at each train station and department store where flocks of people would stand blindly unaware of the masses around them, all calmly awaiting their turn to ride the stairs to the top. These people would subsequently all gather around the tiny connecting floor leading to the next escalator, not realising that collecting in said area was limiting people's ability to dismount the first escalator.

The scene would then be left with a piling group of confused and bewildered individuals, all refusing to use an ounce of energy to move or take any kind of action in order to solve the issue. This then repeated itself at each floor of the train station or department store.

Each time I witnessed this, a mini rage built inside of me and each time I approached an escalator, I would move swiftly into the right-hand lane (as opposed to the left in the UK) and ascend the space next to the snake of squished individuals riding patiently. Of course, riders would stare blankly; confused as to why I had selected to walk instead of queue for five minutes then ride awkwardly to the top. Naturally I was always the first to the ticket gate and skipped yet another pending line awaiting the masses.

The idea for this chapter came from the term ベツベツ (betsu betsu). I first encountered this phrase at a restaurant when it came to paying the bill and a friend asked the waiter "Betsu betsu dekimasuka?" (Can we pay separately?).

I thought this term most useful and added it to the 'Useful Japanese' file on my phone. It would later occur to me that although betsu betsu was welcomed when paying (in some cases), the betsu betsu culture didn't really extend any further than this. The term literally translates to different or separate. It is extremely useful when splitting a bill, otherwise you can just use 'betsu' to distinguish a difference between two things. This really made me think about how things worked back home in the UK and how life there compared to Japan.

Individualism and separation from the masses was encouraged and embraced, yet there was a much higher sense of social segregation and less of a community spirit back home. Perhaps the lack of this in Japan did in fact subliminally aid and expand the feeling of unity, as well as the sense of belonging and togetherness that took place. It is one that was ever present in that overwhelming feeling I experienced when I first travelled there. It's a feeling that's difficult to depict, yet it's one of joy and it always leaves me wanting more; quite like that unexplainable addictive pain synonymous with getting a tattoo.

The sense of togetherness doesn't always extend to situations where someone could potentially become the centre of attention in a public setting, which brings me to the next topic on my list of observations. It comes from witnessing instances where people needed help from others and did not receive it. It's very difficult for me to ignore my instinct to help those in need, and to understand how people can lack such an important innate characteristic.

This isn't to say that people wouldn't wish to help others, but it is such a taboo notion to stand out in a crowded place, that often times, it can appear that people are acting ignorant to what is happening around them, for fear of standing out and being subject of such negative attention.

My first example took place on the train whilst I was on my way to meet friends. An elderly lady stepped on the carriage and in doing so, tripped and fell headfirst into the seats opposite.

Everyone on board simply sat or stood there and stared at the poor woman. I was about to stand up to help when the only other expat, a young twenty-something lad, beat me to it. The woman initially refused assistance, but after realising she was in more pain than she first thought, she accepted this offer. He struggled to help her stand and still onlookers continued to stare. Eventually she made it to her feet and he offered her his own seat. The whole time I could not believe how obviously people were staring and yet ignoring the entire situation. If this were to happen in the UK, multiple people would be rushing to assist where possible.

The second instance again involves an elderly lady on the train who was struggling to stand in the swaying and moving carriage. She was using a walking stick to steady herself but was still stumbling around in difficulty. All this was happening next to the Priority Seats that are clearly labelled in Japanese, Chinese, English and in picture form, stating that these chairs are for the pregnant, ill and elderly.

Each seat was occupied by persons under the age of thirty

playing on their phones or sleeping. It made me mad, so I rose from my seat halfway down the carriage (leaving my bag in place to prevent any other vultures from grabbing it) and walked over to the woman to offer her my seat. The look of shock on her face told me this rarely happened and as she gratefully accepted my seat, the thanks and bows were plentiful. A few stops later a spare seat became available and she signalled for me to occupy it. I gratefully accepted the offer and, for this reason, she became the latest in my string of train buddies made over time.

The third occurrence comes from a Japanese friend's anecdote told to me during my stay there. It is one that took place many years ago when they were on their way out one morning. They arrived at a busy station and entered the packed train. Whilst standing at the edge of the door, waiting for it to close, they slipped and fell through the gap between the platform and the train.

Shouting for help and hanging on for dear life, nobody came to their help and it took them all their strength to clamber onto the platform with bloodied knees and a shaken demeanour. This story in particular shocked me because I could only imagine how frightened and helpless they must have felt and cannot comprehend how people could just stand there and observe.

The final case is one that I have seen a few times, each time different but with the same results: a fight taking place, passers-by stopping to watch and ultimately a foreigner stepping in to break things up. The example I have chosen to depict comes from an article I read about a traveller in Japan. It took place at the West Exit of Ikebukuro station. Two guys had entered a brawl and one was a lot larger than the other. The latter ended up unconscious and bleeding on the floor with the former continuing to attack him at full force. A crowd collected and encircled the pair whilst nobody called for help. It took the foreign traveller to stop, drop his luggage, jump in between the two and shock the attacker for him to consider stopping. The police arrived at the scene but when the traveller tried to offer his assistance, the police refused his help and sent him on his way.

This of course all stems from my own personal opinions and thoughts, and I only seek to make light of these instances, offering a thrilling account of situations that had made me think and question life there. There is also of course a wide expression of individualism found in Japanese culture, music, fashion and in particular in places like Harajuku and Shimo-Kitazawa. There I would find vintage and hipster shops lining the labyrinthine streets, where men dressed as women, and where girls donned their favourite coloured contacts and wacky anime outfits.

I could speak for hours or write an entire separate book on how amazing this country is and how its people were incredibly kind, thoughtful and welcoming. This country will always be my home away from home and I will always cherish my time and memories there. It is for this reason that I chose to write this critical piece to offer an insight into a part of Japan that perhaps people are unaware of, albeit in the extreme minority of cases.

Queues would always continue to annoy me, especially when they're seen as a good sign rather than a deterrent. The ovine traits of some no longer frustrated me and started to amuse me, and I would forever sacrifice my seat on the train for the elderly because that is just the way of my inner British gentleman (which, according to some people, is another debate in itself!).

20

TRAIN CHRONICLES #7

電車物語#7

Girl Power?

Standing on the platform one morning I was suddenly the subject of everyone's attention. Even the station attendant was giving me the eye but was not sure whether or not to approach me. Was there something on my face? Was I doing something wrong? Of course, I was doing something wrong. This kind of silent judgement was synonymous with foreigner wrongdoings, but what could I possibly have done wrong this time around merely by standing patiently in line?

Well as it transpired and was pointed out by the woman behind me, my wrongdoing was what lay between my legs. I was in fact standing in line for the female-only carriage.

Segregation on public transport? Did I wake up in 1950's America? Surely this couldn't be a real thing. Well yes, it was in fact a very real thing in Japan and in nine other countries worldwide, all with the same aim: to protect women from sexual harassment and gropers in such confined spaces.

I wasn't quite sure what to think when this was first brought to my attention. I had both witnessed and fallen victim to sexual harassment in the past but was unaware of its occurrence in a public arena of this magnitude.

Did people truly perform such heinous acts in this wonderful place I now called home? And in public? I'd seen men pushing women out of the way on several occasions to grab the seat before them, but this was a whole different ball game. Unfortunately, the answers I would come to discover were so much worse than I could have ever imagined.

I did some heavy research before voicing my concerns and opinions to those around me about such a sensitive issue, and came to uncover a plethora of conflicting and altogether disturbing information.

I have often heard rumours about *chikan* (gropers/molesters) on the trains, and am profoundly aware that women are subject to negative attention in all sorts of places – like in the workplace and in bars and restaurants, but after learning about the heavy laws and low crime rates within Tokyo, I was apprehensive to believe this still happened on the trains, especially as they seemed such quiet and crowded places. I continued to research further, which drastically opened my innocent and ignorant eyes to the fact that this is the reasons for the female-only cars.

176

Public surveys ran in Japan revealed that almost two thirds of women in their twenties and thirties reported being groped or victimised frequently whilst riding the trains. The train companies stated it is simply impossible to reprimand or catch the perpetrators because they could easily hide amongst the heavy crowds. If proven guilty and caught, gropers could receive a sentence of up to seven years' jail time or a ¥50,000 (£350) fine. Women also stated that they were too ashamed or embarrassed to come forward.

Women-only cars on the trains began many years ago, just after the second world war, but were officially enforced on the Keihin-Tohoku Line, the line I commuted on every day, in 2010 as an official anti-groping measure. There were no legal enforcement or penalties for men riding these cars, it was simply run on a volunteer basis through means of signs and passenger reminders. The rules only took affect between 7:30-9:30am and did not apply to males of elementary age, those with physical disabilities or those accompanying women as carers.

This all brings us nicely onto the worst discovery I encountered during my topical exploration. Japan's answer to fighting molestation crimes on the trains. It falls not in the form of a law or an enforced action, but a café.

In a basement, deep in the winding western back alleys of Ikebukuro lies Tokyo's first Train Café. It claims to be fighting the issue of *chikan* and helping to keep them off the streets.

177

This members-only club charges clients the high fee of around ¥5000 (£30) entry plus ¥2000 (£13) for a mandatory cup of tea with each visit. The young women employed by the Train Café are clad in school uniform or aprons to please the male clientele.

The café itself is decked out to resemble the inside of a carriage on the Yamanote Line (famous for circling the popular stations of Tokyo). Real scenes of the journey from Ikebukuro to Meguro pass by the windows and halt every so often to simulate the passing and arrival of each station. As the real recordings from the trains announce each station, the doors open and young women enter signifying the commencement of the session.

Clients (of which there are around 4000) can touch and fondle the staff however they please as long as they follow the single rule of no ejaculation on the premises. They also have the option to pay ¥4000 (£25) for a twenty-minute session with the employee of their choice. The café employees stated they were proud of its realistic approach to the trains, and feel they have a crime reducing effect.

It has been said that some men have to rush to the café after almost being driven to madness riding the real trains through fear of acting out their lewd temptations. The female staff have also revealed that they enjoy working there because they can make friends whilst acknowledging they will be touched, which is much better than being startled in public.

178

Rather than reducing crime, doesn't enabling such sordid acts in an exclusive club setting ultimately promote their exclusivity?

Shouldn't this side of Japan be made more heavily publicised in order to raise awareness and combat this activity once and for all?

It would be very difficult for me to ignore any such behaviour if I ever observed it first-hand. I would often stand up for the treatment of women in public places and in the workplace if I ever saw or heard anything out of hand. This is one very big and important aspect of western culture that, in my opinion needs to be readdressed and brought to the forefront of conversations in the east.

21

SASUGA

流石

For my second Christmas after coming to Japan I decided to fly back home to the UK for three weeks. I had been away from my friends and family for eighteen months and was well overdue for a visit.

I very rarely suffer from homesickness, but there was definitely nothing better than spending Christmas at home with all my loved ones surrounding me. Landing in the UK and arriving in my hometown, I felt instantly at ease. I knew my surroundings, I knew the people and I was home.

I thought I had planned the three weeks very well, but ended up overbooking and didn't stop for a second to breathe; fitting in different people for breakfast, brunch, lunch, dinner, supper, midnight snacks and the munchies. Why is it we arrange to meet people around various food o'clocks?

It was lovely being able to drive my car once more and not having to rely on the trains. Speaking to people in my native language felt effortless and the most noticeable difference was that I once again had the ability to be invisible. On a day trip to Cambridge with my mother one morning I looked through the crowds of people rushing around in their winter jackets and boots and noticed that no-one was staring at me. No-one looked at me or made a comment as I passed them.

I turned to my mum and announced, "I feel invisible. And I love it!"

It hadn't truly dawned on me how different I would feel returning to the UK after such a long time. Friends had grown, changed their hair styles, moved house, and were now fantastic parents to toddlers. My sister had moved across the country and my parents' house had been redecorated. Local farmland was now bearing signs of the beginning of a housing estate, and new shops had appeared in the town centre.

For the most part, everything else had remained the same. I was able to slot right back into my old life with the friends I had grown up with. I visited an old workplace and past colleagues were still complaining about the same dramas that once haunted my dreams, but now involved new people. Family feuds still existed and I had to remember which family members were talking to which and whom I had to avoid mentioning in certain conversations.

I saw and visited all the people and places I wanted to in such a short burst of time that I ended up having the most perfect holiday home. Had I actually been homesick and not realised all along?

Friends in Japan that had returned home previously, warned me of the plethora of questions I would receive about Japan, and that I would be sick of going over the same information with many different people. However, this wasn't the case for me.

I realised that I didn't mention Japan or my experiences at all whilst home. I would speak to most of my friends and family on a bi-weekly basis so the only thing that was new information to them was how my flight went, and after that was out of the way we could move onto other topics of conversation. My life in Japan felt like a distant dream and I found myself not even thinking about it until it was time to pack and return.

As I bid farewell once more to all my friends, I was surprised to discover that it bore a distinct lack of emotion. My friends had adapted to not having me around and had prepared themselves for the new status quo to resume. As much as I loved them, I had been the one who chose to leave and should have been happier for them. This upset me, and I knew I was saying goodbye to not only my favourite people, but to my favourite chapter of my life, and one I could never revisit.

Arriving at Haneda airport in early January 2018, I felt a strange sense of longing for my friends back home as the tables turned and now the past three weeks felt like a distant dream. I returned to my apartment, unpacked my bags and it was as if I had never left.

Later that week, work began and normality returned but somehow something was different. Small things that never would have bothered me were suddenly like earwigs boring into my brain. The very sight of some colleagues was so abhorrent to me that I reverted to wearing headphones whenever in their vicinity.

Outside of work, passengers on the trains who were once a fascination and addiction of mine were now so repulsive that I couldn't stand to be on-board any longer than necessary. I took to rereading all the electronic books saved on my phone just to distract myself during these arduous journeys.

Friends would invite me to exciting outings and events and I declined or ignored them all, simply because the thought of forced fun and false jollity would irritate and become a burden before I had even left the house.

The silly rules of Japan that I once found endearing would enrage me just out of the pure audacity and ignorance they projected.

Why wasn't everything the same as the UK? Why was everything suddenly so different and frustrating? Why did I miss my friends so much?

Wherever I went, something, someone, somehow, would annoy me for no particular reason and I just couldn't understand why. I stopped initiating conversations with my friends back home and the longer they didn't message me, the angrier I became.

Didn't they care about me? Had I finally become old news? Didn't we have fun over Christmas after all?

Looking back on this part of my stay in Japan, I can see that this was all in my head and complete nonsense, but at the time I was not (for lack of better words) a happy bunny. Six weeks after I returned to Japan, it took an intervention from a very close friend in the UK and two friends in Japan to snap me out of my stupor.

Dan and Rhianna took me to a local haunt, our favourite sushi bar, one evening and shook out of me (in a very heads-on approach) what was going on in my mind. I told them how I had been feeling and after all the initial concerns and advice, the instant response from Rhianna was, "Sasuga!" (as one would expect).

It was as clear as day to her what was wrong with me as she simply revealed that I was currently undergoing the second wave of the dreaded culture shock. She told me everything I was thinking and feeling was completely natural and to be expected returning home after such a long time.

"Excuse me? I went through this whole ordeal last year. You mean to say there's a second wave?" I asked.

Well, apparently, yes.

I was warned of reverse culture shock upon returning to the UK, and had half expected to experience it then, but seeing that I skipped this stage, I didn't expect to be hit with a healthy dose of it once back in Japan. They both explained to me that they had also experienced similar feelings and thoughts when they returned, which was soothing to compare and contrast.

After a quick round of research, it appeared that the diagnosis was in fact spot on. Being presented with a label and an explanation to decipher my everlasting case of the grumbles was a huge relief, and I felt a tad lighter at once. They made me promise that I would not be a stranger anymore and the three of us made a pact to be more open in the future.

I contacted my friends back home to see how everyone was doing and whilst I had been stewing over and cursing everyone for abandoning me, they had just been living their own lives. Raising beautiful babies, buying houses, changing jobs and attending university. As life happens, time stops existing like it did when we were at school, and we picked things up from where we left them. Nobody had realised how much time had lapsed and all was well.

I returned to work the following week with a new attitude. I would turn up, do my job and leave work at the door. Any communication with co-workers would be strictly professional and that would be that. The company was undergoing many big changes and transitions, and I didn't wish to get sucked into the inevitable drama that would naturally ensue.

This new outlook on life changed me for the better and allowed me to see things from the other side. Culture shock is a strange phenomenon that can occur at any time and for any trivial reason. It is a very unique feeling and is one I should be able to recognise should it strike again in the future. Well in theory, that is, anyway, but here's hoping.

22

TRAIN CHRONICLES #8

電車物語#8

Invisible

It was a beautiful Saturday morning in Ikebukuro. The sun was low and the shadows long. The light breeze in the air was perfect and I felt snug in my shorts and t-shirt. I had nowhere to be and nothing to do; the afternoon was an empty abyss. I walked with a sense of ease and comfort, for this city was mine and I felt like discovering something new. People were gathering around the west exit of the station, more people than usual. There must have been some kind of function or event on. I began to walk in its direction, hoping whatever it was would peak my interest.

It was a book fair. Interest peaked.

The courtyard was organised into a semi-circle of pop-up tents displaying and selling books from all eras and across all genres. I sauntered slowly through each tent, passing manga and novels of all kinds, history and science books, and stopping at the antiques. I adore antique books and pictures. Boxes upon worn boxes were full to the brim with school pictures and family portraits that sparked images of Victorian horror movies. There were small boxes of faded train ticket stubs and stamps of all sizes and colour. I could easily have spent all afternoon perusing through each at my leisure.

I noticed some art prints sticking out between two musty books and as I pulled them gently, a pile tumbled out all over the stall. I had hit the Ukiyo-e gold mine (a traditional style of Japanese art). I began to rummage through each one before anyone else could get their greedy mitts on them, and discovered one I was fond of. I have always had a fascination for Ukiyo-e but was put off by the extortionate price of the prints. I slowly and hopefully turned over the one in my hand to check the disgusting cost and was stunned to discover it cost just ¥100 (70p).

'Could this be right? No time to question it, buy it before anyone else realises the error,' I ran over in my head.

I purchased it at once and rolled it neatly to place in my bag for safe keeping. The sun was now beginning to set, so I decided to start heading home. It had been a good afternoon and I was delighted with my haul.

At the station, I began to climb the stairs to my train line and could barely make it onto the platform. I had never seen this line so crowded in all of my time in Japan. Perhaps there had been an accident or a delay. Or perhaps the hot weather had drawn out more people than usual.

The train slowly pulled into the station and I noticed the passengers shoved up against the windows; packed in like sweating sardines. No-one got off. Great. People waiting on the platform were now assuming the squeeze and push technique, attempting to force their way onto the train. I gave up and decided to wait for the next.

It arrived two minutes later and was in the same state.

'Abort mission!' I thought at once.

I tried a different line. This one arrived significantly less packed, but by now people had caught on to the idea and were stampeding towards the rapidly filling train. I was swept away in the current and my choice of direction was immediately stolen from me as I was dragged further onto the train. I guessed I was there for the stay.

The jingle played and the doors closed. Everyone adjusted themselves around me to reach for a handle or railing. I found myself in the dead centre of the train, equidistant from every possible surface. I was completely surrounded with nowhere to move. I felt the heat emanating from seven complete strangers, each rubbing up against me as the train swayed over the tracks. The taste of flatulence filled the air and I scanned the scene for signs of a culprit. What could I do? I physically could not move. My thoughts turned to my beautiful new Ukiyo-e print hanging by my side in my tote bag.

189

'Please survive this ordeal,' I prayed.

The human tumble dryer intensified with each passing stop, and as people forced their way out, more people got on. I was now wedged up against the glass of the door and had just one more stop to endure. Luckily the doors opened on this side and I could sashay out unscathed.

I was forgetting one thing. I had decided to ride a different line. The doors now opened on the opposite side. Joy.

The train arrived at Akabane and surprisingly I was the only passenger in the entire carriage who needed to disembark. This never happened. Akabane is a hugely popular transfer station. I was going to have to run through the Japanese train tactics if I wished to leave this vehicle in time.

Tactic one: shuffle my body towards the door to notify those around me that I am preparing to leave. For some reason, this didn't work. Was I missing something?

Tactic two: the push. Didn't work.

Tactic three: the "sumimasen" (quietly say excuse me to those around me). Didn't work either. What was wrong with people today?

Tactic four: the slightly louder "sumimasen". It was like I didn't exist.

Tactic five: shout "SUMIMASEN".
Nope. I was now being stared down by dozens of disapproving eyes. And the conductor was announcing the closing of the doors. Well, at least I finally had everyone's attention.

And for the finale, tactic six: scream "MOVE OUT OF THE WAY!" If all else fails, shock them with English. Suddenly I was Moses parting the Red Sea.

My bag got caught on somebody as I leapt off the train in dramatic fashion. I yanked it out but milliseconds before the door closed on a carriage full of bemused passengers.

Well that was an ordeal.

The moral of this story: if all else fails, never underestimate the power of English.

And to answer the burning question in everyone's mind, my print made it out with just a tiny crease in the top corner: a worthy war wound for my feat of a beautiful summer's afternoon.

23

KOMOREBI

木漏れ日

Golden week is a collection of public holidays that makes up almost the first week of every May. The whole country is on vacation, and I saw it as a good excuse to leave the hustle and bustle of city life and plan a vacation away somewhere. In May 2018, along with Hannah and Owen, I elected to visit Nico in Okinawa, Japan's version of Hawaii.

We spent the week exploring the tiny southern island, visiting all the tourist spots and fitting in some well-deserved beach days and night time swimming.

We took a mini break for a couple of days, and rode the ferry across to the tiny island of Tokashiki. As we approached the island I was overwhelmed by its uninhabited nature and the rising rock formations bursting out of the ocean. Covered in moss and tropical flora, one could only imagine what else dwelled in this potentially unexplored terrain. I felt like John Hammond and couldn't help blurting out in my most British accent, "Welcome… to Tokashiki

Island!"

With our newly sea-swept hair and a taste for adventure, we began our island voyage with optimism and high spirits.

The following morning, we travelled to a beach twenty minutes away and decided to have a beach day. Walking through the streets towards that dip in the skyline that can only signify the presence of the sea, we saw through a hole in the trees our first glimpse of the ocean up close. All shades of blue and green merged into the most beautiful natural colour I have ever seen. How could a body of water look so tranquil and stunning? I just wanted to take a running dive into its midst, soaking up all the nutrients and feeling revived from within.

There wasn't a cloud in the sky and we were surrounded by huge rocks and boulders that formed caves and walkways through the scenery. Coral seabeds rising out of the sand below lay passage from each rock to the next, and the imminent sense of adventure overtook me.

It was decided that we would go for a quick dip in the sea to (pardon the pun) test the waters before any exploration missions were executed. The water was perfect. The soft sand below caressed my toes as they flexed against it for traction. Most importantly, I could see all the way to the bottom so there were no surprises looming in its depths. Entering the sea in the UK is always a gamble, for you never know if you're going to tread on a crab, glass bottle or dead seagull. But this, this was something else.

After a brief spell in the sea, Hannah and I went on a rock pooling excursion to explore the caves upon the horizon. We spotted many curious creatures on our hunt; tiny iridescent blue fish darting away from our shadows, long legged spiky star fish waving out of every crevice just below the water's surface, small fluffy creatures that I just wanted to pick up and squish (we later discovered they were in fact the aptly named Teddy Bear Crab) and mudskippers bouncing joyfully from rock to rock.

A few hours later, we returned to continue lounging in the heat before the sun began to cast its long shadows and retire for the evening. Upon changing and packing up our belongings, it was brought to my attention the new colour of my feet, for it seemed that wading through the shallow waters had removed any sun lotion applied earlier. What were once golden-brown feet were now swollen red paddles with bold white flip-flop lines.

Perfect.

The following day was our last on the island and we decided to go snorkelling in a different area recommended to us. Arriving, we soon realised that we had the entire beach and lagoon to ourselves. Some of us hired snorkels, masks, flippers and life jackets, myself included. Everybody was already in the sea as I sat on the water's edge attempting to squeeze my now painful and red raw feet into the cold hard rubber flippers. I breathed through the pain and waddled backwards like a disoriented penguin into the sea.

I am not the strongest of swimmers and it took me a while to get used to breathing in a new fashion. Becoming suddenly conscious of how to breathe was a strange notion in and of itself, but slurping in bits of salty water then projecting them back into the ocean with one deep exertion every few breathes was most annoying. I'm sure I was doing it wrong.

I took my time, taking in my new surroundings and becoming gradually accustomed to floating like a buoy lost at sea. Every now and then the others would call over to check I was still alive, and I would offer a hearty wave in return.

As I lowered my face to the surface of the water, I entered a whole new world (cue the Disney song) unknown to me. Highways of coral reefs and crowds of exotic marine fauna bustled about below; all moving with purpose and going about their day uninterrupted from the world above. My presence didn't seem to bother anybody in the slightest and I felt a sense of Big Brother syndrome as I peered into the lives of those around me at will.

Surfacing once more to check my bearings and clear out my goggles, I saw something large and dark just to the right of me. Assuming it was a huge chunk of coral, I attempted to fight the current and avoid collision. The waves carried me towards the mass as I fought even harder to move away.

Or was it now moving towards me? It couldn't be. Could it?

I donned my goggles once more and quickly resumed my buoy position. Swimming directly below me, casually and fully at home in his underwater utopia was the most beautiful creature I have ever laid my eyes upon. A young green turtle was now gliding effortlessly through the water mere feet from where I was floating. I heard myself scream with shock through my snorkel, and the turtle raised an eye to look in my direction.

We swam like this for thirty minutes or so, and as the turtle foraged below I marvelled in its beauty and majesty. It drifted close to me several times; allowing me to run my palms over its carapace and stroke its head. It didn't seem phased by my presence and we both shared this special moment together unscathed and uninterrupted.

It was at this point where I suffered what I like to think as the most millennial moment in my entire adult life. The battery on my camera had run out and I was forced to make an impossible decision.

Do I stay here and fully embrace this moment, just being fully submerged in nature and all its wonders? Or, do I return to land to swap over my battery in the hope of returning to the exact same spot as my new-found friend to document it?

Hannah had caught up by this point and after reeling in the moment for so long, I decided to risk it and swam at full speed back to the beach. I instructed her that she follow the turtle no matter what.

Returning with fully battery power, I met a small group of people, along with Hannah and now Owen who had caught wind of what was happening. We swam alongside one another once more and I captured some beautiful footage that I can now look back on with fond memories.

Finally surfacing after a while, it dawned on us that the sun had disappeared and the temperature had dropped drastically. I peered down once more and the turtle had vanished into the now misty depths below. I looked to the shore and the man who ran the snorkelling hire shop was standing by the water's edge shouting for us to return because the sea was becoming too dangerous. Looking around I could feel the waves getting choppier and we began to struggle towards the beach.

After what felt like a lifetime of swimming one pace forward and being dragged twenty paces back, I reached the shore completely exhausted, and as the water pulled at my swimming shorts, I felt something heavy weigh my pocket down. I nervously put my hand inside and recognised at once the touch of my phone.

Shit!

I barely had a second to accept that my phone was no longer before, through the howling winds and rustling trees, came the sound of a girl screaming. The four of us were present, but a girl who had joined us for the day was still in the sea. Running to locate her, it was soon apparent that something was dreadfully wrong.

Running up the beach clasping her arm, she announced to us that she had been stung by a jellyfish. Earlier on that day we had been warned of the presence of the deadly Portuguese man o' war jellyfish in the surrounding seas.

Frantically grabbing our possessions, we quickly ran to a nearby hotel in full panic mode, dripping from head to toe all over the foyer. We demanded that she saw a first aid trained employee, and they rushed her into the back room and deduced that it was a sting from a non-fatal species. Thank goodness she would be ok.

Once we knew she would be fine, I asked with one last desperate ounce of hope if I could perhaps borrow a hairdryer for my phone. I sat in the corner of the entrance way, soaking the chair and floor around me, shivering from the air conditioning, attempting to dry my waterlogged and, let's face it, completely dead phone.

How could such a fantastic and exhilarating day end with such a sense of loss and frustration? I am usually so careful with all of my possessions and had nobody to blame but myself. Thus began the month-long stint without a phone. I now had no way to contact family or friends back home (those of whom were not on social media that is), but part of me kind of liked the idea of such distance.

I usually tried to experience life in real time but had definitely succumbed to living through my phone's camera lens on many occasions. I rarely went anywhere without my headphones and my music playing as it drowned out the sounds of the city and distracted me from the multitude of people at close contact on the trains.

What was I to do now?

I left all technology at home each day and instead carried around a book. A real paperback book. I read most days but being in Japan could prove difficult to locate cheap English books so I usually resorted to electronic books on my phone. Reverting to paperbacks felt so lovely and listening to the sounds of the city after so long added to the atmosphere of living in Tokyo.

Not being fixed to a device allowed me to once more appreciate the little things in life, people-watch freely and wholeheartedly and take in the sight and sounds around me.

Watching Studio Ghibli movies during my time at University, I would always notice how nature and light played a heavy part in the overall feel of the story. I began to notice this is real life as I walked through parks. The trees there stood differently, and the way the light filtered through the leaves, painting a dappled light show on the ground, brought on a sense of catharsis.

Komorebi. This wonderfully created word described this sense perfectly. There is no translation in English which I like because it feels like a very Japanese term. It refers to the eloquent effect of sunlight that streams through the leaves of the trees. The shadows cast on the ground describe this beauty.

Living for a month completely off-grid whilst out of the house was a truly marvellous and liberating experience. No longer was I a slave to the device, checking it every ten minutes and relying on it solely for time, directions and entertainment. I would come across a beautiful sight or a funny scene and would stop and enjoy it, revelling in the moment. Childhood nostalgia came flooding back in the most mundane of situations because I was now living in simpler times. I was free.

When the day finally came that I would receive my new phone, it was an anticlimactic one. I loaded up my new master and all the messages I'd missed over the previous four weeks came flooding through like a tidal wave. I spent the next couple of hours responding to them and checking my social media feeds.

I tried not to rely wholeheartedly on my phone from then onwards for everything in life. When I returned home each evening, I would keep it on silent and put it by my bed. I truly believed I wasn't so engrossed in technology until this ordeal took place and shocked me into reality. From then on, I made sure to actively appreciate the finer moments in life, and to remember every now and then to channel my inner turtle and just be.

24

TRAIN CHRONICLES #9

電車物語#9

Ray of Light

One Saturday in May, I attended a regional speech contest for high schools in Tokyo. I had spent the past few weeks coaching and mentoring one of the students through her speech and went along for moral support.

Initially, I wasn't particularly enthusiastic about spending an entire day listening to kids preach about their favourite idol groups or how we need to build more Disneylands, but as soon as the first student opened her mouth, my opinion changed completely.

Five hours of speeches later, I was simply blown away. These young students had somehow produced the most innovative and mature speeches, all discussing topics that are so important within today's society.

One young man opened up about how he grew up in Japan,

and studied in America for a semester as a junior in high school where he was integrated into school life. There, he learned to think freely and voice his own opinion in lengthy and healthy debates. Upon returning to Japan however, his classmates scorned at his new-found extravert demeanour and would physically attack him at any opportunity.

This physical and mental torment continued until one day when he simply couldn't cope anymore and he attempted to end his life by jumping off the school roof.

He expressed in his speech his concern at how people in Japan react and treat 'haafu' ('returnees' - people with one Japanese parent) or non-Japanese citizens. Racial discrimination and discrimination of those who are 'different' is a huge problem that needs to be addressed more often, so it was refreshing to hear this brave young man discuss it so openly.

Many of the other speeches discussed similar racial and cultural topics, from poverty to the entertainment industry. One girl very bravely voiced her discord towards allowing foreigners into Japan. Her justification for this was that non-Japanese people residing within the country are taking all jobs and homes from the Japanese, are making Japan a dangerous place and are a general burden. This was met with a lot of uncomfortable shuffles and head shaking from the many non-Japanese teachers sitting in the audience.

The girl who spoke last left an impact and resonated with me as she chose to speak about the LGBT+ community, with emphasis on the taboo surrounding it within Japan. She regaled us with anecdotes from her time studying abroad in Australia where she described her fellow classmates as being happy and open with their sexuality.

She noted that people in Japan were ashamed and afraid to embrace their sexual orientation and instead chose to ignore it. She said students need to feel safe exploring their sexuality and shouldn't have to hide who they are. Classmates and teachers alike should offer support and the schools shouldn't put so much pressure on students to conform to the social 'norms' deemed acceptable.

I had personally witnessed this all too much living in Tokyo. I had met so many men who were married with children and who spent every Friday and Saturday night in the bars and clubs of ni-chome, Shinjuku's LGBT+ neighbourhood.

Upon asking them how they felt living this way, the answers always seemed to be of a similar nature: they didn't need to be happy because they had to be married or have children. Sometimes their wives knew about their second lives, and as long as it was out of sight, it was out of mind. I couldn't imagine having to live this way in a permanent state of unhappiness.

It took me coming to Japan to finally accept who I was. I learned how to feel content and confident with the person that I am, fully embracing it for the first time in my life. At first, I thought it was because I was away from everybody I knew, and could reinvent myself as it were, but I then realised it was because I didn't feel judged here. I felt like I could express my individuality and the fact that I was gay didn't matter; nobody there would bat an eyelid. So, I began a new chapter of my life, one I would never go back on.

It wasn't until I would go out in the evenings and interact with other people who identified the same way, that I realised I was the lucky one. My experiences of notifying the people who mattered to me the most was nothing but a positive thing. 'Coming out' is gradually becoming a thing of the past in the west where same-sex marriage is mostly accepted and the community is starting to be represented well in the media, but in Japan it is still very much a country that is deep, deep in the closet. The very notion of standing out is inconceivable and should be suppressed.

After the speech contest, I left with a friend feeling emotionally exhausted. We spent the evening laying on the grass of Minami Ikebukuro Park, thinking over the day and positively analysing each speech. We felt a sense of pride for each student that presented, and it left us with high hopes for the future of this nation. If the next generation continues to progress socially as we witnessed at the contest, this Victorian way of thinking would soon be a thing of the past. This is the ray of light I needed to see.

Sitting on the train on the journey home, I continued to reflect on the day's proceedings. Feeling ever more positive about what I had heard, I began looking around at the passengers on their evening commute home. I began to wonder how many of them had felt similar feelings and thoughts to those kids from earlier on that day. How many had suppressed their true selves or lived separate private lives from their friends and families.

In this moment, my eyes were drawn to a man standing opposite me. His posture and balding head told me he was perhaps in his late forties, and it was clear he had obviously had a long day and was ready to dive into bed. He was holding onto the handrail by the end of the row of seats and was fighting to stay awake. Every now and then his other arm would raise and slap ceremoniously on his quite portly beer belly, the hollow sound resonating around the carriage.

I peered down towards his feet and in doing so, noticed his tanned trousers had a dark stain just above his knee. I followed it up and found that his entire crotch was also dark with the same stain. And it was getting bigger.

Oh dear.

I was the only person in the train who had realised we were in the presence of a man expressing his bladder all over himself. Thankfully, my station was coming up, and I would be making a swift exit very soon indeed. I had to chuckle to myself as I once again reflected upon the day I had just had. What a huge contrast.

Well I guess Rome wasn't built in one day, and just like Rome, Japan surely won't change in a day, but there's still hope yet.

25

DAIJOUBU

大丈夫

Daijoubu is one of my favourite Japanese words and it is by far the most useful word I encountered in daily conversation. It could be utilised in almost all situations, especially when I was unsure how to answer a question or request, and wished to avoid reverting to English. Daijoubu has several uses and meanings, the most common ones being: "It's OK", "I'm OK", "That's OK", "Are you OK?" or "No thank you".

I often used daijoubu in my daily life, but one particular occasion will forever be synonymous with the term whenever I hear or use it.

It was a scorching hot day during my Golden Week vacation to Okinawa with Nico, Hannah and Owen. I was zip-lining through the trees with a group of close friends. We decided to partake in some adventure sports for the day as it would be a good experience to do so over the jungle-esque flora.

Health and safety were of course pivotal for our survival, and we were in charge of our own welfare, clipping and unclipping the carabiners accordingly. I made sure I had my friend double check I was securely attached before taking any swinging leap.

It took us a few hours to zip from tree to tree, climbing ever higher through the canopy whilst working together as a team, ensuring we all made it to the end unscathed. After the initial fear, it felt kind of liberating, soaring so far above the ground without a care in the world.

The final challenge came in the form of an obstacle course on stilts. Swings, roped bridges and hooped steps were waiting to be manoeuvred in order to make it successfully through the course and reach the final zip line to the ground thus ending the day.

Halfway through, attendees were required to climb up a very steep rope ladder and clamber onto a tall wooden podium. After attaching myself to a new rope suspended in mid-air, I was expected to take a risky leap from the post, freefalling somewhat and finally swinging into a net standing parallel to the podium. I had to then climb up the net and continue on with the course.

Simple. Right?

Before we reached this part of the course, we would discuss at length how fun and simple it looked, never worrying about the pending doom. Upon reaching the post, I watched two of my friends casually take the jump and rejoice on the other side at how much fun it had been. It was then my turn.

I gingerly made the ascent, pulling myself up and over the ledge to stand before the young instructor waiting to assist. I looked down and was suddenly overcome with fear. Not a fear of heights, a fear of falling from them.

The older I become, the more fearful of death or things that could kill me I become. This was one of those situations. As a kid, I would have leapt freely as a bird without any fear of injury or demise, but here I stood, frozen to the spot like a rabbit in headlights.

I expressed my fear to the instructor, who swiftly assured me with a gesture that I had another option. I could in fact descend back down the pole and take the easier route across a small rope bridge. The children's route as it were. I'm not afraid to admit when something frightens me, but this was more about overcoming the obstacle and achieving this feat together as a team.

The longer I stood there the deeper my thoughts went into realms of 'what ifs'. What if I should plummet to my death? What if the rope doesn't quite hold and I break my legs? What if I jump in a weird way and end up hanging myself? What if the harness pulls too much and castrates me? All very important questions.

The final friend in our group waited patiently behind me and offered words of encouragement. From across the other side of the cavernous abyss, the remainder of the team shouted across further cheers and advice. Then I heard a soft voice behind me for the first time. The instructor announced in an inspiring and calm manner, "Daijoubu desu". "It's OK".

He wasn't sure if I could understand Japanese or not, but he felt that he needed to offer some words of wisdom to make me feel that everything was going to be all right.

For some strange reason, this had the desired effect and it pulled me out of my nonsensical stupor enough to distract me from my current predicament. I decided to take this situation and the resources available to me, and formulated a logical plan of action. I asked the instructor if instead of jumping, could I sit down on the edge of the podium and fall off. This made perfect sense in my head and would lessen the impact of the fall.

He agreed that it was ok so I began to lower myself down. It was at this point that I realised the rope wasn't quite long enough to create the optimal effect. This then brings us to one of my finer moments.

In an awkward squatting position, with my hands wrapped around a very taut rope that was now causing extreme discomfort in my nether regions, I persisted to lean forward and very sadly (and not so triumphantly) roll from the podium into the abyss.

In what felt like a lifetime, but in reality, was but a few

seconds, the rope caught me as planned and I swung into the accompanying rope opposite. Climbing up the rope, I heard claps and cheers from my group as the final member made his way onto the podium.

I relived the entire moment once more in the seconds it took me to climb the rope, and recalled that strong feeling in my chest like my heart would drop out via my bowels as I pathetically plunged in what can only be described as a proud foetal position. This recollection brought a smile to my face as it gave me the drive to cheer on the last in our group. He attached himself, jumped, swung, grabbed and climbed up to meet me in under five seconds.

Simple.

We all ended the course on a high and with a huge sense of pride for each other. We had achieved something great, even though it was always going to be a safe and happy adventure. We felt like we'd gained something very special, and most significantly, we'd done it together.

Later on, I thought back to the podium and why it was so difficult for me to manoeuvre, but also more importantly why I refused to take the easier route. Then it hit me; it's the same with any big decision in life.

When I'm at a crossroads, facing two big decisions, do I take the easy option or do I take the hard? Sure, one is more convenient than the other, but one can also be seen as the cop-out route, the bypass route. Life decisions are never easy and it is the fight and strength that goes into them that makes them all that more special and worth it. If I plan on settling for convenience, will this also inevitably welcome regret and unhappiness? Will it welcome a sense of failure and lack of achievement?

I am a strong believer in taking leaps of faith in working towards a goal or aspiration. Before coming to Japan, I was faced with a similar scenario: do I stay in a secure job where I'd worked my way up through the ranks, or do I risk it all and start all over again from scratch? It was a tough decision but it paid off massively. Leaving said job was the best thing I could have ever done for myself and I feel that I earned it even more because of the risk involved. Putting myself out of my comfort zone is never easy but sometimes in life it's completely necessary.

So, with all this behind me, I took the leap, both off the podium and in life. I had decided to follow my gut and ignore the easy way out. I had decided to take the long path and work my way towards the next chapter of my life. The next chapter that would lead me into the unknown even further; into new surroundings with new rules and cultures; into a new life, and out of Japan.

26

GAIJIN

外人

One sunny morning in June, I was crossing the road at a
junction by my house where there were no cars in sight and
many people waiting for the next round of green lights. I
was in a hurry and the light was not quite red so I made an
informed decision and ran for it, just making it as it turned
red.

I heard a loud grunt from behind and turned to see an
elderly man waiting on his bike. He was pointing
aggressively at the light to inform me I had made a grave
error in judgement. The light was still green and I raised
my arm to shrug him off and continued on my path. The
lights made a full round and turned green once more. As he
passed me on his bike he shouted yet again in my direction.
I ignored him until I clearly heard the word, "GAIJIN".

He waved me down and put his finger to his head to signal
that I was a mentally insane. "GAIJIN". Meanwhile,
neighbours and local shop owners alike, all of whom I
would pass and greet on a daily basis were now stopping to

212

watch. The man who owned the bike shop had just opened his mouth to wish me a good morning and was now standing awkwardly as the cyclist called attention to me. Fifteen people who were all heading towards the station stopped to stare at the "GAIJIN".

Had this gentleman called to inform me that perhaps I should have waited for the next green light in a polite manner, I would have apologised and that would have been that. But he shouted aggressively and I saw no justification for his verbal attack.

Neighbours and people among my community had now singled me out as a bad person and I was met with stares of judgement and disdain, all because these people would rather stand by and watch than support and stand up for one another. I was the bad guy in this situation.

As is clear from the rest of this collection of stories, Japan is a uniquely different place like no other, and each time I visit, I become more familiar with certain customs, rules and traditions. I am aware of cultural differences and how oftentimes visiting foreigners will be treated with celebrity status. They are followed around by interested onlookers, receive special treatment because they're different, and quite often the foreigners themselves take advantage and learn to "Gaijin Smash".

The kanji for gaijin literally means outside (外) and person (人) or to put it into one word, foreigner. The polite form of this is gaikokujin 外国人, or outside country (国) person.

The word gaijin can have negative connotation attached to it, or can be used as a slang form of the former. Whatever the case, living in Japan I would encounter this word on a daily basis either from strangers or other foreigners using their foreign status to cheat or smash the system. Thus, the term 'Gaijin Smash' was born.

Visiting Japan in the past, I became accustomed to the stares and comments from strangers as I stood out like a sore thumb with my huge backpack, camera and, before buying a smartphone, map.

Living in Japan was very different because I commuted to work every day wearing my smart attire. I didn't walk around with a camera and map as my sidekick. I wasn't amazed or excited by vending machines and temples, or seeing tourists driving Mario Karts around the city like maniacs.

I adapted and became accustomed to my new life and I tried to fit into society the very best I could. I studied Japanese and attended classes in my spare time to improve communication with the locals, and I followed all the rules down to a tee, however silly they may have seemed.

As touched on previously, I began to realise after a while that all this effort seemed to be going to waste and that whenever I would go out to eat, the restaurant staff would give me the English menu or insist on speaking to me in English. Shop attendants would ask for my passport each time I purchased something of value so they could stamp the tax-free form for me to pass over at the airport. I would tell them in Japanese that I lived there and they would reply in English saying simply, "Thank you".

Strangers approaching me to take my picture, or stopping to ask if I were lost, when I was clearly walking at full speed with meaning, began to wear thin. I would especially dread the inevitable look of panic I received every time the tables were turned and I needed to approach somebody myself.

It was as if I could hear their brain ticking over: "Oh no, I must now enter English mode. What was that grammar point I studied in high school? I can only remember the words for 'cute' and 'see you'!"

I carefully prepared what I needed to say, and asked a question very slowly in Japanese. The look of panic would appear and the receiver did one of three things:

1. Replied in Japanese saying 英語湧かない (I don't speak English)
2. Replied in English either perfect or broken (even though I had displayed Japanese competently)
3. Ran to find someone who spoke English with whom I would repeat my question in Japanese

This is a concept that is extremely foreign to us in western countries. First of all (and I hope I'm not just speaking for myself here), when we encounter people of other nationalities, we do not instantly panic and assume they are not of this land or do not speak English. Second of all, we do not start randomly speaking another language in the hope that we have selected the correct one. I had seen so many (non-British) Europeans saying to Japanese people in broken English, "Sorry, I don't speak English."

So, because of all of these facts, it was very difficult to progress and be accepted as a resident; for I would be reminded on a daily basis that I was different and therefore could not possibly comprehend the Japanese language or culture.

This began to bother me somewhat around the time I was deciding whether or not to remain in Japan for a third year. Would I continue studying everyday if I was unable to utilise my new-found knowledge? Would I feel at home if I were reminded daily that I was in fact not? These questions followed me around and would rear themselves during times of vexation.

This brings me to just a few examples of scenarios that happened to me over the course of my stay there. I need to premise this with the statement that these attitudes were not those of the masses, but these are examples that stick out in my mind. There have been so many incredible bouts of generosity and kindness that I will always cherish, but for now I am taking a more serious turn.

The small-minded attitudes of so many people are that of over 100 years ago, and I have had my fill of it for one lifetime. The fact that I was constantly reminded that I was 'different' on a daily basis was one thing, but to be outright shouted at in public was another.

To recap, I had been pushed up against the train door with "GAIJIN" shouted in my face. I had been rejected from renting apartments because I was a "GAIJIN". I received multiple phone calls from my management company telling me there had been a breach in the rules and it must be me because I was the "GAIJIN". I had been denied access into my own apartment through a path I used every day, and when trying to diffuse the tension get shouted at by an elderly woman calling me the "GAIJIN". Then there was the time I crossed the road (heaven forbid).

The evening following the abuse from the man on the bicycle, I went out for dinner with Dan and Rhianna. It had been a long time since we were all together and we decided to go to a pizza buffet. We had just finished lining up to get our food and as I walked past two young men, heard one of them exclaim to the other very clearly in Japanese, "There are too many foreigners in here!"

I put my plate down, turned around and walked right up to them to say as clearly as possible in Japanese, "I understand Japanese!" Their faces immediately turned a shade of scarlet and they bowed in shame as I walked away.

It's a sad feeling when something you cherish so much is suddenly tainted and tarnished with darkness. They say you should never meet your hero and I understood this through discovering people's true intentions and thoughts. This was especially true the longer I lived there and the better I was at understanding the language.

No matter what I did, how I acted, how I tried to sink into the shadows or blend into society, I would always be different. Not because of something I had done as an individual, but because I was a GAIJIN, an ALIEN, a FOREIGNER.

I had never been the kind of person to assume that racial discrimination was cause for any altercations witnessed, and I certainly never thought I would experience it just for existing. Now, that is a concept that I would gladly deem as FOREIGN to me.

My favourite book has always been To Kill a Mockingbird, and after reading the highly anticipated second book Go Set a Watchman, I remember feeling slightly let down by my hero.

Atticus Finch had always been a hero in my eyes; the perfect gentleman who saw the world for what it was. No dramas, no judgement, just a calm and collected individual. But when it was revealed in the earlier drafts that he had a different character altogether, this broke my heart.

I left this book alone for a couple of years and would reread the former during my stay in Japan. This copy has become a bit of a security blanket, and I take it with me on every trip. I decided to give Watchman one last read with fresh eyes, and was blown away at the similarities I felt between reading this and living in Japan.

Japan was my Atticus.

Something I had almost worshipped and looked up to with the utmost of respect had been forever tainted in one swift movement. I would never look at it the same again.

Upon further reflection, I looked to the narrator Scout for more answers. Mockingbird was written from the perspective of her six-year-old self, full of the innocence and naïveté of a child.

Watchman was written from the perspective of Scout in her late twenties and her eyes are opened to the reality of the world she grew up in. Her father, her idol and God, is broken down layer by layer to reveal the man inside.

I used this same sense of discovery to explain the cause for my second wave of culture shock and my sudden discovery of the real Japan. This was not a bad thing in the slightest, but I felt I put so much emphasis on the utopian state of Japan that I may have misread and misjudged things along the way. I allowed my own naïveté to cloud my mind to things I simply didn't want to see and hear.

These experiences most certainly shaped me into a better person, and I felt a sense of clarity and understanding of the world a bit better after living there. My encounters and interactions were all significant and added to the knowledge and wisdom I gleaned from each individual.

219

Of course, everyone was different and Japan is without question a polar opposite to many countries in the west, but it was how I reacted to these situations and what I would learn from them that was most important.

So, the next time I would fall victim to the inevitable GAIJIN attack, I would of course react accordingly, but also take a second to appreciate the cultural differences, to understand the ignorance and lack of exposure, and do my best to rectify the situation as best I can.

27

TRAIN CHRONICLES #10

電車物語#10

Talisman

Tanabata festival is celebrated every year on the 7th of July. It is also known as the Star Festival, and celebrates two deity lovers who meet one another once a year if the skies are clear. Towns are adorned with bamboo trees covered in paper wishes, as paper floats and streamers sway from above. People clad in yukata and kimono fill the streets, buying food and drinks or playing games from the many stalls.

It is a fun celebration for all and for many it marks the start of a new summer season. For my second year in Japan, I visited Asakusa with a group of Tokyo based friends to partake in the festivities.

Warabi was also hosting its own festival the same day, and beforehand I noticed posters hanging around the train station to advertise that their festival had something to do with the celebration of trains. The poster also pictured local merchandise being sold, including a keyring of the Warabi train station sign. I thought this would be a lovely souvenir of my time in Japan so decided to stop by on my way to Asakusa.

At the station that morning, I came across a stall selling the goods and was pleased at the prospect of picking up the keyring without having to attend the festival itself, especially as it turned out that it was being held at an elementary school.

Immediately diving towards the box of keyrings, I searched frantically for Warabi, but could only see the neighbouring stations of Kawaguchi, Urawa and Nishi Kawaguchi.

Asking the clerk if they had any Warabi keyrings, he regretfully told me that they could only be obtained through being won in the raffle. I stood there for a minute, looking forlorn, deciding on whether I should enter the raffle and risk winning an oversized inflatable shinkansen or barrel of train toys, or should I try to beg for the chance to purchase one.

As I stood there trying to figure out the correct vocabulary to ask if they could go against the system, I overheard the two clerks engaging in a conversation about me. They were saying how badly they felt that they couldn't give me the keyring, especially as I was a foreigner so was probably visiting, and therefore wanted a souvenir.

222

I mean, they weren't completely wrong, but if it meant I would obtain the keyring, I went with that.

I asked the woman how much the raffle was, pretending that I hadn't just understood their conversation, and she responded with the price of a ticket. I gave her the money and she sneakily placed the keyring into a paper bag, handing it to me with a motherly grin. I bowed to them both and thanked them for their kindness before continuing my journey.

The Tanabata festival was a real hit. Hordes of visitors from all over attended and the sun was out in its fullest. The vibe was that of fun and jollity and the very best of Japan revealed itself for this one perfect day.

As the sun set, I bid farewell to my friends for the evening and returned to Warabi, stopping by the supermarket on the way home.

Walking up and down the aisles, I was approached by a young Japanese man who asked me if I was Kurdish. This took me aback as I was not expecting this kind of interaction or question out of the blue. I told him that I was British.

He responded with, "But you're in Warabi right?"

"Yes," I answered, slightly confused.

"Have you not noticed all the Kurdish people?" he asked.

"Erm… yeah I guess so." Where was he going with this?

"Well don't you know what us Japanese call Warabi?" he quizzed me.

"I've no idea," I told him.

"Warabi is known as Warabistan by the locals because of the large Kurdish community," he explained calmly.

"Oh. Wow. OK. Isn't that a little mean?" I asked him. I wasn't sure what to do with this information.

His phone suddenly appeared and he asked if he could send me a link to a New York Times article, explaining the term. It sounded quite interesting at this point so I allowed him to share the link.

I went home and read the article. I was not prepared for what I was about to read. This article depicted the current state of Kurdish refugees in and around Warabi. Interviews with some individuals reported that many of them felt lucky to be able to seek refuge in Japan but that Japan wasn't as welcoming as they had expected.

Interviews from Japanese residents claimed that they felt unsafe upon seeing groups of Kurdish residents standing and talking together outside stores, and felt crime rates would increase. They said they feared jobs would be taken from Japanese residents too. Some Japanese citizens had a positive view on the situation, but unfortunately this opinion appeared to be of the minority.

Reading this article and the first-hand accounts from Kurdish people residing in Warabi made me empathise with them. I was fortunate enough to hold residence status but could relate especially when it came to the discrimination.

This was the true dichotomy between living in Japan and travelling there on vacation. I felt a sudden sense of closure after reading the article. I finally understood the catalyst for all the verbal abuse I had received over my time there.

I always thought it strange how when I would compare stories with other friends living in Japan, they hadn't faced half of what I had, and would often wonder why we'd had such different experiences. Was it just me? Was I more perceptive to these things?

And now I knew. It was my surroundings.

I wasn't sure what to make of this. The place I'd come to love and call home was suddenly an entirely different place. I know ignorance is bliss, and that plays a large part of being a foreigner in Japan, but this was too important to ignore.

I decided to rise above the negative views of some and continue to go about my days as I had been, but a little more informed. I would stop and correct those who I overheard talking out of line about foreigners, particularly within

Warabi, because perhaps they were misinformed and awareness needed to be raised.

This inspired me to teach a class at my school about the issues surrounding foreigners in Japan. The class was met with first shock and disbelief, but then warmth and welcome responses from the students, and they would go onto thinking about it at great lengths. They would then begin to notice real life situations they would have otherwise missed, and this sparked important and mature conversations between them and other teachers. It was a first step in the right direction and I was proud to have achieved such a miniature personal feat.

I would always cherish my Warabi keyring, because after all the train escapades and dramas and adventures, I felt I had become accustomed to the madness that was the Japanese train journey. It would forever remind me of how much I have overcome and that no matter how people see or perceive me, I must always remain true to myself. I didn't expect to think in such a cliché manner, but would now carry my tangible 'Train Chronicles' talisman with me wherever I went, and it would be carried with pride.

28

OTSUKARESAMA DESHITA

お疲れ様でした

Mt. Fuji

Otsukaresama deshita is a staple term that graces every aspect of Japanese culture. I would hear it at the end of every working day, every club meet, every day trip or any activity that required an ounce of labour, be it physical or mental.

Loosely translated it equates to: "Thank you for your hard work", but the sense of pride and achievement that would come from it was tenfold of its English counterpart. I really felt a part of something and it made all my efforts worthwhile to be acknowledged in this age-old fashion.

The last time I both used and received otsukaresama deshita during my time in Japan was on my final big adventure. I had decided not to recontract and would leave Japan after two years of living there. Before I left I would need to complete the final item on my 'Japan Bucket-List'. The one thing I'd been putting off until the timing was right, and what better time than a week before I leave?

Destination: Mt. Fuji.

Along with Dan, on what was to be our final adventure together, I boarded the early afternoon bus from Shinjuku to Mt. Fuji's 5th station. The morning was already a scorching one and temperatures were growing into the mid to late thirties; typical for the end of July. Wearing running shoes, shorts and t-shirt, and carrying a backpack full of warm clothes and important supplies, we set off on what was to be the longest and most worthwhile journey of our time in Japan.

Leaving the 5th station at 15:30, the gravel path started off pretty levelled, lined either side with horses feeding off the dense vegetation, and in the centre, teams of youth, elderly and all in between hiking at full steam ahead like in an army drill.

We had purchased wooden walking sticks adorned with the Japanese flag on top. This was to be our souvenir and saviour of the day. There were many stopping points along the way and each offered a branding stamp service for the walking sticks. Each depicted the location and the altitude along with a local character or deity. They also brought with them a mini feat and sense of achievement for each leg of the hike.

The path soon changed from soft fixed gravel to harsh loose

rubble and volcanic debris. The inclination increased at a rapid pace and the strain on our legs intensified.

We reached the 6th station after a while and were met with a collection of small wooden huts dimly lit by warm lights and steam emanating from inside. Selling snacks and warm beverages at high prices, the inn keepers greeted us with earnest personalities and beaming smiles. A sign for the toilet explained that there was a fee of two hundred yen to use the facilities.

At around 19:00 the sun began to set and as we turned back, we noticed the ever-rising mist had caught up with us. A trail of bobbing lights wove its way up the mountain side, and as our eyes strained to focus on the mass, we realised that it was a human caterpillar (pop culture forced me to avoid use of the word centipede) of elderly individuals marching their way towards the summit.

Not wanting to get caught up in the mass, we donned our head-torches, climbing gloves and winter attire and continued up past the 7th station, high into the night. The terrain became increasingly steeper and transformed into jagged coral like rocks that with one wrong footing would send us spiralling back down the mountain. We had to start using our hands to grip onto the volcanic rock and hoist ourselves further upwards. There was little space to stop and rest, so stamina was pivotal during these intense moments. Yet we continued to push ever onwards.

Reaching 3400m at around 20:30, we noticed the shining

beacon of katakana letters reading トモエ high up in the night sky. Our stop for the night. At last we reached Tomoe-kan, our cabin for the evening. Seeing the sign and the thought of a hot meal gave us the energy boost to push forward for the last few hundred metres.

We dined on katsu curry and were ushered into our room/attic crawl space. Our wooden-beamed metre-high quarters were just tall enough to crawl into and sitting up was impossible. Futons lined the floor and at our feet were boxes of water bottles and cabin supplies. A small ladder stood at the head and this was our entry into our nest for the evening.

Managing only an hour's sleep, the shuffling of the other guests woke us around 01:00. We joined the masses and prepared for the early morning ascent. We were given bento boxes of salmon and rice for breakfast which were consumed right away for that well-needed energy boost, as we joined the flock of lights ascending into the dark like spirits all traversing the same collective pilgrimage.

For the final leg of the journey, the terrain became even more dangerous as we ascended higher and higher. One small woman walking in front of me fell backwards twice and would have rolled right past me had I not caught her bag handle and lifted her up onto the rocks in front.

At last, the summit presented itself around 03:30. I looked over at Dan and was met with a face full of tearful emotions and a huge sense of accomplishment. We hugged one another and congratulated each other with a hearty, "Otsukaresama deshita". We walked among other exhausted climbers all huddled together for warmth in preparation for the sunrise. Over all the heads, we could see the famous Fuji summit vending machine selling hot drinks at very high prices.

Finding a secluded spot on the side of the summit, we stopped and set up camp for the 04:37 sunrise. As we sat waiting, the freezing temperatures began to settle in our bodies, and it became harder to focus on anything other than staying warm.

There weren't many people present at this time and looking around, the scene was so peaceful and serene. This fantastic event that occurs every day without fail, in this moment, was all ours. 04:37 rolled around and the first beams of light began to peer above the clouds we were now standing over. Suddenly the temperature was not a problem anymore and we simply sat and marvelled in the majesty.

Hues of yellow, orange and red began to emanate the scene. The clouds embraced new light with open arms as the two danced in joy, forming fluffy new shapes and structures with each passing minute.

We took the standard tourist pictures, received the final stamp on our walking sticks and began the long journey back to the base.

The path down was nothing like the way up. The route was

very steep and the terrain was that of loose rocks and thick dust and ash. The views were monotonous and feelings of progression were non-existent. We were forced to stop regularly to remove dust and debris from our shoes until the 5th station welcomed us back with open arms at 10:00.

Wow. We did it. We tackled and accomplished Mt. Fuji. Our walking sticks were covered in branded achievements, and the sweat on our brows and rumble from our stomachs confirmed the feat.

As we settled in a nearby café, the two of us reflected upon the past twenty-four hours, and the feelings and overall struggles were not that dissimilar from that of the past two years living in Japan. We had experienced highs and lows, moments of pure joy and moments of pure exhaustion; all the time progressing towards one goal.

I think the emotions we displayed at the top were heightened by the fact that this hike was subconsciously symbolic of everything we had overcome whilst living in Japan, and that our time here was finally coming to a close.

This excursion was the final agenda on my 'Japan Bucket-List' and I could now leave Japan, proudly knowing that I have ticked it off and achieved the ultimate final challenge.

CONCLUSION

結論

I spent the first week in August 2018, and my final week in Japan, saying goodbye to friends and co-workers, and doing all those boring things necessary when moving country. I had to visit the city office to hand in my moving out notification, dismantle and carry all my furniture down four flights of stairs to leave on the pavement for the ward office to collect and recycle, clean my apartment from top to bottom and move into a friend's apartment for the final few days.

I had to pay for my entire apartment to be remodelled (new floors, new wallpaper, six new tatami mats) despite the fact that it was all in immaculate condition. All that along with the fees to remove all of furniture and cancel my bills ended up costing me a total of around £3000 which was ridiculous and non-negotiable. Just to leave my apartment. Sasuga Japan!

I treated myself to a final haircut and an acupuncture session, and became a tourist once more as I visited all of my favourite places for the last time. Harajuku, Omotesando, Akihabara and my favourite sushi restaurant.

Riding my final train to the airport, I wondered what dramas may unfold, but for once it was calm and all was well. This gave me time to reflect upon my time in Japan. All the highs and lows, all the crazy adventures and cultural experiences, the many nights in and even more out, the subtle exchanges between complete strangers and the lifelong memories with great friends.

Japan allowed me to openly accept and be myself for the first time in my life. After first discovering the difference between travelling to Japan and living there, I was worried that I had been exposed to a world I wasn't ready to accept, and the ideal was tarnished. But after a while my relationship with the country plateaued into what it now is, and the country in essence became my Atticus Finch.

I came to Japan with an empty diary that turned into my wonderful Journal of Firsts which ended up becoming my first book. This amalgamation of the old, new, familiar and strange inspired me to take written notes and accounts of the profound, bizarre and amazing.

Stereotypes I was once privy to altered as the mystique of this country unfolded and revealed itself for what it truly was, and I was forced to accept some harsh truths along the way. I felt that after a long time of reflection, I could safely part Japan as old friends with no qualms, regrets or concerns.

This has been by far the best thing I have ever done and it

was a long time coming. I will always cherish the fond memories and know whenever I hear a certain song or eat a certain food, I shall forever be reminded of the crazy adventures I have embarked on. I very much attach important memories to songs that I hear at the time, and have a plethora of song memories to draw happiness and inspiration from.

There were so many beautiful nuggets of culture interwoven into everyday life that people simply took for granted. The sweet potato man that went about his day with his high-pitched siren, the women wearing elaborate kimonos, the men bowing in excess to their bosses, were all special events that I used to notice upon arrival. Sitting in the staff room on my final day of work, I remembered my first week there and that feeling of discovery and that anything was possible. During that moment, I realised I didn't even notice those things anymore, until someone new would visit and ask me about them.

"But why is it that way?" they'd ask.

"It just is," I'd answer. "Because Japan."

ありがとう日本、本当にお世話になった。じゃ、また
ねっ！

Thank you, Japan, for looking after me. Well, I'll see you!

A Note from the Author

This book has been two years in the making and while it has been a huge learning curve, I truly enjoyed the long nights of soul-searching and early morning epiphanies. I never set out to write a book, but after sitting down to journal my thoughts, what I ended up with was the first draft of the thing you now hold in your hand. Whether directly or indirectly, many special individuals have aided this book's creation in one way or another, and I would like to extend my eternal gratitude to you for making this lifelong goal a reality.

To Terry Lack for your never-ending guidance, mentorship and for the priceless journal that started it all, to Chloe Barnard & Deepash Bhavsar for your kind hospitality and giving me the space to write, to my Japanese sisters Chiaki Oda & Eri Ozaki for helping with my never ending questions, to Dan White & Rhianna Whitwell for all the crazy adventures and for making my time in Japan the most magical experience, to Marco Giovannini for starting me on the path to publishing, and to the following wonderful people for your kind support during my campaign: Leanne Bolsover, Melinda Bowman, Nicola Bragg-Hart, Julia Emms, Hannah Lane, Caroline Le Grys, Stavros Milionis & Patrick Nall c/o Darcy Farquaad, Polly Monk, Annette Poole, Lana Ringer, Nico Schilling, Noriko Shibatsuji and everyone at Takinogawa Girls School, Karen Smith, Ben Southam & Kelly Southam, Ian Thompson & Nikki Thompson, Tegan Vorley, Andrew Watson & Kate Watson, and Owen Wren.

BV - #0005 - 040820 - C0 - 197/132/13 - PB - 9781912964338